ALTBIER

ALTBIER

History, Brewing Techniques, Recipes

HORST D. DORNBUSCH

Classic Beer Style
SERIES no. 12

A BREWERS PUBLICATIONS BOOK
Boulder, Colorado

Brewers Publications, Division of the Association of Brewers
P.O. Box 1679, Boulder, CO 80306-1679
(303) 447-0816; Fax (303) 447-2825

Printed in the United States of America
10 9 8 7 6 5 4 3 2 1

ISBN: 0-937381-59-4

Copy Editors: Anna M. Huff and Kathrin Rueda
Interior Photographs: Mark Duffley and Horst Dornbusch

Direct all inquiries to the above address.

Library of Congress Cataloging-in-Publication Data
Dornbusch, Horst, D.
    Altbier : history, brewing techniques, recipes / Horst D. Dornbusch
      p. cm. — (Classic beer style series ; 12)
    Includes bibliographical references and index.
    ISBN 0-937381-62-4 (alk. paper)
    1. Ale—Amateur's manuals. I. Dornbusch, Horst D. II. Title.
III. Series.
TP578.D67   1998
641.8'73—dc21   97-51327
                                         CIP

Those who are completely mired in the past are irrelevant reactionaries who fail to comprehend the human potential of the living. Those, on the other hand, who dismiss the past as old-fashioned bunk are arrogant fools who must not be trusted. Only those who preserve and transform the past and make it come alive in the present are part of that organic whole we call civilization. In this spirit, this book is dedicated to all those anonymous brewers who, at home or on the job, have kept the altbier faith alive over the centuries and have thereby enriched our sensory world and enhanced our human experience.

Contents

Foreword

By Herbert Enderlein

He who drinks it for the very first time might experience
its true delight only after the third or fourth sip. We are
referring to the spicy, bitter Düsseldorf altbier. To Düssel-
dorfers, this top-fermented beer is a drink from the gods.
—Former Düsseldorf archivist Dr. P. Kauhausen in 1950

Dr. Kauhausen's assertion is as valid today as it was
in 1950. It is pleasing to the eye to watch the amber-
colored to dark brown brew cascade straight from a
wooden cask into a cylindrical glass and form a firm,
finely laced, white crown of foam. Swift waiters clad
in blue garb carry the beer to the tables. In the cozy,
comfortable brew houses, steeped in tradition, the air
is laden with history, the living past, and centuries of
artful brewing. There, the captain of industry stands
next to the tradesman, the laborer next to the teacher,
the physician next to the student—social barriers
seem to melt away.

It is important to preserve this culture of the alt,
especially at a time when the world of beer is dom-
inated by "lagers." This is what Horst D. Dornbusch
has recognized as he, through the study of sociology
and politics, discovered his love of beer, specifically

of altbier. With *Altbier*, Horst has captured the history of this old brewing method and has preserved our knowledge of it for posterity.

Herbert Enderlein is the brewmaster at Brauerei Ferdinand Schumacher, the oldest altbier brewery in Düsseldorf, Germany (Schumacher opened its doors in 1838).

Preface

Who says there is no such thing as a German *ale?* Eat your *lederhosen!* If you think the German beer land is just a lager land, think again, *jawohl!*

To be sure, some of the world's finest lagers hail from Germany, but their predominance on the scene of fermented grain beverages has been a relatively recent phenomenon, made possible only by the invention of refrigeration in the late 1800s. Ales, on the other hand, have been brewed in Germany for at least 3,000 years, and probably longer.

Societies as a whole, just like homebrewers as individuals, tend to start out making ales long before they venture into the realm of lagers. In beermaking, therefore, lager is a late bloomer. It was not until the nineteenth century that the lager revolution began to sweep central Europe and, indeed, the world. Faced with a rising tide of bottom fermentation, the Rhineland alone remained the region in Germany that stuck stubbornly with the *alt* (German for "old") method of top fermentation. Alt brewing, thus, has a proud and unbroken tradition that dates back to the beginnings of civilization. Adapted over time, altbier is now made with the ingredients, equipment, and processes available to modern brewers. Nevertheless, it is a piece of living history, one of those rare links to our human past that is not tucked away in a museum but is available and accessible to us all in our daily lives. I am sorry if I appear partial, but I was born and raised in Düsseldorf, the ancestral home of alt. I grew up on this stuff!

By some standards, alt is a most peculiar breed of beer. It is fermented "cool"—warmer than a lager but not quite as warm as a British ale—with top-fermenting yeast, and then it is aged near the freezing point for anywhere from two weeks to several months. In short, alt is a lagered ale. Because of the way it is made, alt represents perhaps the best of both styles: the flavor and complexity of a standard ale with the subtle refinement and clean finish of a lager.

Those who are more familiar with British-style beers might approach alt as a German equivalent of a bitter or a brown ale. Kölsch, the other famous German ale, by comparison, is perhaps more akin to an English pale ale. An alt can range in color from light copper to tan, as determined mostly by the grain bill. Depending on the choice and quantity of hops, an alt can range in flavor from assertively bitter (up to 50 IBU) to decidedly sweet and malty (down to 25 IBU).

In spite of this seemingly broad definition, certain unifying characteristics make an alt a member of an identifiable beer family—a style—that sets it apart from any other fermented beverage in the world. Because of the alt's unique temperature regimen in the fermenter, it must be produced with yeast strains that—though top fermenters of the family *Saccharomyces cerevisiae*—have a special tolerance for colder temperatures. As a general rule, the typical ale yeasts that make wonderful British pale ales, porters, or stouts are singularly unsuited for brewing an authentic alt. While the blonde cousin of the alt, the kölsch, occasionally may be made with a mixture of ale and lager yeasts, this is never the case with an authentic alt.

As a typical German beer, alt is always full bodied. This means alt cannot be made properly by simple one-step infusion. Although decoction is no longer a must with modern grains, multistep mashing is, and all brewers of authentic commercial alts stress the need for a protein rest. If you brew your alt from extract, the choice of malt brand is paramount.

Finding the proper yeast, having the proper equipment for multistep mashing (or the right source of extract), and controlling the fermentation temperature, therefore, are the three greatest challenges facing a North American home- or craftbrewer who attempts to make an alt. This may explain why alt has been relatively slow in gaining acceptance as a beer style in the New World. All too few good altbiers are available in stores, either as local brews or as imports.

If Burton-on-Trent may be hailed as the birthplace of the classic English ale, Düsseldorf on the Rhine is clearly the home of the original alt. Düsseldorf, incidentally, is a mere 44 kilometers (fewer than 30 miles) down river from Köln (Cologne), where the kölsch ale originates. Together, these two Rhenish metropolises, Düsseldorf and Cologne, are the bearers of the modern German ale torch. Although the blonde, Pils-style lager has become the predominant beer style in every other region of Germany, in these two cities the local ales are still the overwhelming favorites.

When a Düsseldorfer says, *"Ein Bier, bitte,"* he or she means an alt, the local default drink. I did not fully appreciate the uniqueness of my hometown's brew until my youthful spirit and itchy feet had carried me far from my cradle. Now that I have tasted beers all over the globe, I have gained my perspective. There is still something irresistible about those lagered ales from Düsseldorf. To me, they will always taste of home.

Acknowledgments

The ancient Greeks held that those who know when they don't know actually know more than those who don't know what they don't know. I am indebted to many individuals, companies, and institutions that have generously contributed to this book, whenever they knew what I did not. Special thanks are due to the following:

Jim Beauvais and Paul Sylva, Principals of Ipswich Brewing Company, Ipswich, Massachusetts, for letting me play with their big buckets until I figured out how to make alt and German lagers as well as British-style beers in commercial-size batches.

Klaus Bell, Braumeister, Hof Aspich, Lahnstein, Germany, for sharing his knowledge of German brew systems.

Scott Brown, Brewer and Partner, Four Corners Grille and Flying Goose Brewery, New London, New Hampshire, for his practical advice.

Steven Clarke, Engineer, Ipswich, Massachusetts, for helping me brew in my kitchen when my alt still had training wheels and for his advice on modifying old refrigerators for lagering.

Darwin E. Davidson, Ph.D., Technical Director, S.S. Steiner, Inc., Yakima, Washington, for his generous advice on hops chemistry.

Chuck Doughty, Brewer and Head of Packaging Operations, Old Nutfield Brewing Company, Derry, New Hampshire, for introducing me to the tricky world of beer-color predictions from grain specs and for letting me use pictorial material from his vast collection of beer labels.

Mark Duffley, homebrewer, Hyannis, Massachusetts, for generously sharing his experience in extract brewing and for cheerfully brewing countless five-gallon and one-barrel batches of alt with me at the H&M homebrewery.

Herbert Enderlein, Dipl.-Braumeister, Brauerei Ferdinand Schumacher, Düsseldorf, Germany, for giving so generously of his time and expert knowledge and for showing me how he makes his alt right there, at Schumacher, in altbier heaven.

Jeff Gendreau, Head Brewer, Ipswich Brewing Company, Ipswich, Massachusetts, for his generous advice throughout this project.

Horst Genten, homebrewer and fellow expatriate from the Rhineland, now living in Osterville, Massachusetts, for making me feel welcome, weekend after weekend, in his "modified" garage (known as the H&M homebrewery), which became the research-and-development site for this book.

Acknowledgments

Toni Knapp, Publisher, and Theresa Duggan, Book Project Editor, both of Brewers Publications, for suffering my perfectionist antics with grace and aplomb.

Dave Logsdon, President, WYEAST, for sharing his secrets about the taming of the eukaryote (yeast).

Michael Sova, President, New England Brewing Systems, Gloucester, Massachusetts, for fabricating just the right brew systems for authentic German-style beermaking.

Stephen Torosian, Ph. D., Research Associate Professor, Microbiology, University of New Hampshire, for checking my material about the elusive subject of water chemistry.

Michael Vits, Braumeister, Brauerei Uerige, Düsseldorf, Germany, for allowing me to spend a day in his brewery, where he makes Uerige Alt, one of the great alts in the universe.

Introduction

Lots of books about brewing are now available in homebrew shops and from catalog houses. Some take a strongly theoretical, scientific approach that links the chemical, botanical, and microbiological characteristics of your ingredients to the reactions that occur in your mash tun, kettle, and fermenter. Such books ultimately tie these characteristics to the technical specifications of the beer that results.

This book takes a different, perhaps less demanding, approach, concentrating instead on the more practical challenges of making a German alt authentically. Although I occasionally digress into the realm of science, such treatises are confined mostly to the appendices at the back of the book. You can skip these scientific digressions and still understand the book's practical explanations. When I do use terms such as *proteolytic conversion* or *beta-amylase,* it is simply because no colloquial equivalents exist. On the whole, however, this book communicates in plain English. It is intended to introduce altbier to readers who are generally unfamiliar with the style.

Altbier starts with a quick outline of the history of alt brewing, then explains the flavor profile, ingredients, equipment, and processes associated with an authentic alt. But do not feel compelled to read every word. Go for what interests you, get your brewing paraphernalia ready, and find out whether this beer's for you.

Hurried brewers will probably go straight to chapter 6, the one with the recipe guidelines, which contains a condensed version of the alt-making process. Analytical readers might dwell on the more technical facts and on the variations in the practices of commercial alt makers as outlined in chapters 3 and 5. Tinkerers and equipment lovers will probably enjoy the details about mechanical systems provided in chapter 4. Finally, contemplatives might savor chapters 1 and 2, while sipping a craft- or homebrewed alt.

In this book, I avoid the term *recipe* in favor of *recipe guidelines*. This may seem a small semantic departure from convention, but I believe it is significant. Especially regarding a less common beer such as an alt, the term *recipe* can be misleading. Brewing is not like cooking: "Take half a cup of flour, three eggs, a quarter cup of milk . . ." In brewing, the result can rarely be captured by rigid prescription. The result too often depends on the nature of the ingredients available (grain, yeast, hops, water) and on the process capabilities of the system in which you use those ingredients.

Every brew system has different, innate extract efficiencies, for instance. Likewise, different combinations of grains and hops yield different hops utilizations. We usually assume that 30% is a good approximation of the amount of alpha acids that is eventually carried into the finished beer, but, depending on the age and quality of the hops, the grain's protein level, the mix between complex and simple proteins in the wort, and the physical conditions of your kettle boil, this figure can vary dramatically. Also, we may formulate a grain bill for a certain target color value and then fail to obtain the right flavor.

Megabreweries have a scientific staff and large labs to analyze their ingredients, batch by batch, and to obtain reliable empirical data about the performance characteristics of their equipment under different conditions. Craft- and homebrewers rarely have the skill, knowledge, and facilities to do the same. But you can still make good beer at home or in a craft-brewery, even if you are not an expert in the "hard" sciences of chemistry, botany, and microbiology, provided you understand the interplay among the different ingredient and process variables that affect the outcome of your brewing efforts.

Scientists refer to this interplay of factors as multi-colinearity. This book tries to help you understand the characteristics of your target beer, the alt, and the brewing guidelines that influence how well you can hit your target. *Altbier* tries to help you intelligently manage your brewing's inherent multicolinearity.

Make your first altbier and evaluate it qualitatively. If you are not entirely satisfied, look at your variables and at our guidelines; adjust your ingredients and procedures; and try again, and again, and again.

Achieving and replicating a quality brew is a constant struggle, even for the most accomplished professionals. For instance, you may have made a beer that fits your target specifications exactly. Then you change your grain supplier and . . . the beer tastes completely different. What went wrong? Chances are that the new maltster employs a different kilning technique. While the first maltster may have achieved the color of its grain by a slow drying process at a relatively low temperature, the second may have achieved the same Lovibond rating by a faster drying process at a relatively higher temperature. The first grain imparts no toastiness to the brew, whereas the second does. The effect: two otherwise identical beers, brewed according to the same "recipes," taste completely different.

Great brewing is a true art, not just the mindless application of scientific principles and automated processes to a fixed set of raw materials. Take heart and go for it! If you master the art of brewing an alt, you can brew any beer!

CHAPTER 1

Altbier throughout History

In modern Düsseldorf, it's still *comme il faut* to imbibe in that age-old brew, the alt, whose roots date back to the beginnings of European civilization. *Alt* means old—an allusion to the old style of brewing, before lager.

It seems appropriate that Düsseldorf has become the guardian of the old German ale tradition. After all, it was in one of Düsseldorf's suburbs, called Neanderthal, that, in 1858, scientists stumbled upon the skeletal remains of a prehistoric man, whom they dubbed Neanderthal man. This fellow and his clan were ancestors of modern humans. Neanderthals roamed the Rhineland some 50,000 to 100,000 years ago. Obviously, Düsseldorf has been a busy place since time immemorial.

Two views of Düsseldorf on the Rhine, one from 1585 and one from modern times.

It is doubtful that Neanderthals, who were hunters and gatherers, brewed beer. But their descendants did, probably no later than by the end of the Bronze Age, around 1000 B.C. By that time, Germanic tribes in the forests had started to make ales from grains that grew wild in the forest clearings. Brewing became such an important part of their daily lives that they wove brewing lore into their sagas and myths. We can glean a hint of the importance of beers in those old Nordic societies from one myth, called the *Kalevala*, which has some 400 verses about beermaking but only 200 about the creation of the world. The Germanic tribes thought of the sky as a giant brew kettle where Thor, the god of thunder, was the brewmaster. When Thor noisily cleaned and polished his kettle, there were lightning bolts, and when he boiled his wort, there were clouds.

Early Germanic ales were almost black. They were "mashed" from half-baked loaves of bread made from coarsely ground grain. The grain's enzymes, which we now know convert starches to fermentable sugars, were probably activated during the partial baking

of the moist loaves. Today, we achieve the same effect by malting our grain, drying it in a kiln, and then moistening it again in the warm mash tun.

The Germanic tribes crumbled their bread and then soaked it in crocks filled with water. They often flavored their brews with wild herbs and honey and then waited until the mixture fermented spontaneously. The beer that resulted from this process must have been fairly murky and sour, and full of floating husks and crumbs. (The Alt Mead featured in chapter 6 is a free-style attempt at immitating this tribal brew with modern ingredients.) It would take another 3,000 years of experimenting before Germans learned to make the clean, crisp ales we know today as altbiers.

Because those Germanic tribes were illiterate, we had to wait for the Romans to provide the first written account of Germanic beermaking. At the height of their power, these Mediterranean wine drinkers ventured across the Alps in their quest to subjugate all the inhabitants of the then-known world. The

Romans began to occupy the Rhineland in the century preceding the birth of Christ and discovered a drinking culture based not on the grape, which was unknown in central Europe at the time, but on grain.

The best description of tribal Germanic drinking habits comes from the Roman historian Tacitus, who wrote in A.D. 98 that the tribes "serve an extract of barley and rye as a beverage that is somehow adulterated [presumably he means fermented] to resemble wine" and that they "cultivate the grains of the field [for beermaking] with much greater patience and perseverance than one would expect from them, in light of their customary laziness" (Hellex 1981). Tacitus

obviously did not share today's prevailing view of Germans as hardworking and industrious people.

In Germanic tribal households the man grew the grain, but the woman did both the cooking and the brewing. A maiden who could count among her dowry both a cooking pot and a brew kettle was considered a great catch. The Romans, on the other hand, considered beer an inferior drink and introduced the grape to the Rhineland, so that, on their campaigns, they could imbibe in the manner to which they were accustomed.

As happens so often when two cultures meet, after the initial rejection of each other's achievements, eventually cross-fertilization occurred. The Germanic tribes learned to make wine from their usurpers—and Germans still produce wonderful Rhine wines today—while the Romans learned to brew beer. We know that the Romans had become accomplished brewers by the third century, as is evident from the discovery in 1983 of a complete Roman brewery near the Bavarian city of Regensburg, on the banks of the Danube. The design of the kiln and mash tun suggests that brewing techniques in the Germanic region had by then evolved from the primitive bread beermaking of the Bronze Age to the mashing of malted grains that we still practice today.

During the next five centuries, the influence of Rome over central Europe gradually declined and a new social order emerged in the region we now know as Germany, based on feudalism and the new religion of Christianity. Monks and nuns, who ran their cloistered communities much like extended families, continued the tribal household tradition of brewing. As they were usually among the few well-educated and literate members of their society, they took a scientific approach to brewing. They experimented with new techniques and ingredients and kept systematic records of the results. In the process, they discovered hops as a bittering and preserving agent—though nobody is quite sure exactly when—and probably developed the first German beers of consistently high quality. As the demand for monastery and convent beer increased, so did the size of their breweries. Some brothers and sisters began to specialize in brewery work and became the first professional brewers in Germany. *And all the beer they made was ale.*

The feudal lords soon joined the cloistered communities in the brewing trade, and many a nobleman started his own court brew house (*hofbräuhaus*). The aristocrats, however, more interested in profits than in the art of brewing good beer, were generally less successful in the trade than were the monasteries and convents. Court brewers used not only barley, wheat, rye, and oats, but even millet, peas, and beans in their mash tuns. To cover up off-flavors, the noble ales were often spiced with such unspeakables as pith, soot, chalk, the content of an oxen's gall bladder, or hard-boiled eggs.

Especially in Bavaria, the production of low-quality beers eventually gave rise to a host of beer regulations and decrees, culminating, in 1516, in the now-famous all-Bavarian beer purity law, the *Reinheitsgebot*. It stipulated that only barley, hops, and water may be used to make the brew. Yeast had not yet been discovered. The Reinheitsgebot is the oldest, still valid food-quality law in Germany.

Until the invention of refrigeration in the 1870s, our ancestors could not brew what they wanted, but only what nature let them. Only gradually and by trial and error did they gain a true understanding of fermentation and then realize that the cellar temperature influenced the type of beer that resulted. It would take centuries of scientific discoveries to unravel the secrets of fermentation. The beer that the Reinheitsgebot originally sought to regulate was probably, unbeknown to the medieval Bavarian brewer, a lager during the cold winters in the foothills of the Alps, but it was most certainly an ale in the summer. We can assume that the ales were fermented in part with wild yeasts and were all too frequently infected with bacteria. Thus, for the Bavarian beer drinkers, these summer ales must have been unpleasant brews more often than not.

Not knowing the cause of the drop in beer quality during the summer, the Bavarian rulers decided, in 1553, to outlaw summer brewing altogether and to restrict the official brewing season to the time between St. Michael's Day (September 29) and St. George's Day (April 23). From spring to fall, brewers had to seek alternate employment. It is obvious that this kind of brew schedule favored the production of lagers. Because of the climate, Bavarian brewers simply could not have been making ales in the winter.

The importance of these two regulations—the Reinheitsgebot and the prohibition of summer brewing—is crucial to understanding German beer history. These edicts caused a split between a new lager culture in the south and the old (alt) ale culture in the north. In the centuries that followed, Bavarian brewers perfected their lagers to a point where these brews were able to conquer virtually the entire world. Lagers are now *the* dominant beer style of the globe.

In the north of Germany, where the Bavarian rulers had no say and where summers were cooler, ale making continued. There, the monks and nuns were soon joined in the brewing trade not by nobles but by enterprising city burghers. These merchants were often linked in trading associations—most prominent among them the Hanseatic League—and employed free, wage-earning tradesmen organized in professional guilds. These commercial city brewers were the first secular professional brewers in Germany.

Initially, city brewing, like country brewing, took place mostly in the home. But as fires became an ever greater public hazard in the crowded blocks of wooden houses, many city fathers eventually outlawed not only homebrewing, but home baking as well. They built communal stone bake-and-brew houses in which every household had to take turns making its daily bread and its daily beer, often for a fee. It soon became apparent to the city folk, however, that it was much more convenient to hire staff to run these breweries. Because bakers were already familiar with the raw

materials for beer, they were often the ones chosen to supply the community with both solid and liquid bread. Many a city authority was only too eager to grant to the bakers the exclusive right to make beer and to run taverns where tradesmen and burghers alike could congregate and pass their evenings over a mug of freshly brewed ale.

Cities were the centers of commerce in the medieval world. They provided the ultimate challenge to the feudal lords and their official state, which was based mostly on agriculture. In the end, cities became "free." They obtained charters from the nobles that granted them the right to make their own laws, mint their own coins, levy their own taxes, and run their own commercial and political affairs without interference from the nobles. By the end of the twelfth century, the city burghers and their councils in northern Germany had gained virtually total control over the brewing industry within their city walls and, like the nobles before them, they often reserved the exclusive right to brew for themselves. Thus, ale making, while all but outlawed in the south, became linked with powerful commercial interests in the north: those of the rising class of burgher-merchants and patricians of wealth.

Significant for the history of altbier and its Rhenish ale cousin, the kölsch, was the struggle between the burghers of Cologne and their archbishop over the brew privilege. By the middle of the twelfth century, some Cologne burghers had started civil ale breweries to compete with the monastic breweries controlled by the church. The archbishop, in an attempt to "divide and conquer," tried to regain his former monopoly (and the profits that came with it) by restricting the right to brew, sell, and dispense beer to only a few of the city's patricians. The chosen few agreed among themselves to become specialists in either *gruit* beer (*gruit* is old German for "herb") or honey beer (hops were not yet in wide use in the Rhineland).

The city council, not wanting to be shut off from the revenue the brewing trade offered, managed to persuade the emperor to grant it the right to levy taxes on the finished beer. However, Cologne brewers already paid sales taxes on their malt and excise taxes on their kettles. They had become the heaviest-taxed inhabitants of the city, and it was time to fight back. By 1254, they had founded their own guild (which was officially incorporated as the Fraternity of Brewers in 1396). It regulated the profession and defended the consistency, quality, reputation, and profits of the local beer.

The guild then became a closed shop. It set workmanship guidelines, standardized the training of apprentices and journeymen, issued master certificates, regulated advertising and competitive practices, defined membership criteria, specified wages, determined production quantities, looked after members in need, and punished violators of the guild's rules. Members met at their guild houses to discuss their professional, political, and economic concerns.

In 1288, the brewers took the next step in their fight against the archbishop and his regulations by joining a military coalition of burghers and guilds against the archbishop. They took advantage of an ongoing territorial dispute between the secular political rulers in the Rhineland and the expansion-minded archbishop. The coalition's leaders were Duke Adolf V, ruler of the Duchy of Berg, the rising secular power in the Rhineland, and Duke Jan Primus of Braband and Flanders, a friend and patron of the brewers' guilds of Brussels and Leuven (in present-day Belgium). On June 5, 1288, they led about 6,000 soldiers in a march on Worringen (outside Cologne) in what turned out to be one of the bloodiest battles of the Middle Ages. By the end of the day the archbishop's forces were thoroughly routed and Duke Adolf emerged as the supreme power in the Rhineland. Henceforth, the burghers and brewers of Cologne could brew whatever beer they wanted, without interference or taxation from any greedy archbishop.

Duke Adolf V of Berg decided to create a permanent counterbalance to the might of Cologne by starting a new city about two dozen miles down the Rhine.

On August 14, 1288, he granted a little hamlet by the name of Düsseldorf a city charter. For the next few centuries, Düsseldorf's population slowly increased, until the new city became the seat of government for the House of Berg and started to give Cologne a run for its influence—and its beer.

The earliest mention of brewing in Düsseldorf dates from 873, when the archbishop of Cologne conferred the brew right upon the convent of Gerresheim (now a suburb of Düsseldorf). By the middle of the fourteenth century, records show that a growing number of commercial baker-brewers were plying their trade in Düsseldorf, usually in *keutebier*, a viniferous-tasting brown ale made mostly from wheat.

We know from the land-tax register of 1540–41 that there were 35 brewers in the city at that time. Beer had become enough of a public concern that the local duke, Wilhelm III, imperial elector and head of the House of Berg, issued a police ordinance regulating the quality and price of beer served to his subjects. He also imposed severe taxes on beer brought in from outside the city, thereby favoring consumption of the local ale.

In Cologne, too, the local ale found its protectors in high places, when, in 1603, the city council decreed that only top-fermented beers could be produced in Cologne. From 1607 onward, only ales approved by the city council were permitted to be poured in

Cologne. Thus it happened that only some nine decades after the Reinheitsgebot had become the law in Bavaria and pushed that part of Germany firmly into the lager column, the authorities in the Rhineland took quite the opposite course by giving their top-fermented beers, their ales, an exclusive market.

In 1622, a bakers' and brewers' guild was consti-tuted in Düsseldorf. As we know from the 1632 land-tax register, the house at Bergerstraße 1, the present-day home of the famous altbier brew-pub Uerige, was shared by a baker named Martin Pütz and an innkeeper named Diederich Pfeilsticker. The founder of the present brewpub, Hubert Wilhelm Cürten, too, was a baker with brewing credentials. He got his brewery license in 1855.

The rulers of the House of Berg were not only the protectors of the local brewing trade; they were also great consumers of the local ale. In 1695, the Elector Duke Johann Wil-helm even built his own court brew house, whose ales were reserved solely for his Eminence and his courtiers. If the Bavarians could have a purity law for their bottom-fermented beers, so

Duke Johann Wilhelm, atop his mighty steed, still dominates the old marketplace and city hall of Düsseldorf. He ensured the purity of the local ale by issuing the Düsseldorf Reinheitsge-bot. This bronze statue was cast during the duke's lifetime by the Italian artist Chevalier Gabriel de Grupello.

could the Rhinelanders for their top-fermented ales, or so the duke decided in 1706, when he proclaimed the so-called Düsseldorf Reinheitsgebot. It, too, required that only barley, hops, and water were to be used in a Düsseldorf ale.

In 1709, Duke Wilhelm strengthened his beer-quality regulations by insisting in a police ordinance that "nobody may tap a cask that is not at least several days old, is bright and well-sedimented" (Rümmler 1985). To raise professional standards among Düsseldorf brewers, he licensed the first Düsseldorf guild for brewers only, in 1712. The new guild started out with 57 founding members. By 1768, it had grown to 94.

The guild came to an abrupt end in 1797, when French troops under Napoleon occupied the Rhineland, including Düsseldorf and Cologne, and Joaquim Murat, the newly instated governor and brother-in-law to Napoleon, forbade all trade and professional associations. Napoleon suffered his crucial defeat at the Battle of Waterloo in 1815, and the Rhineland was given to Prussia at the Vienna Congress that same year. But the Prussian rulers confirmed the abolition of the guilds, arguing that their closed shop had been too restrictive by depriving the new Prussian citizens of their freedom to choose their profession or trade in open competition.

One feeble attempt at a lager takeover was made in the Rhineland in 1830, when the banking dynasty of the Rothschilds decided to invest heavily in a large, state-of-the-art brewery for bottom-fermented beer in Cologne. The brew, however, turned out to be substandard, because the cellars lacked adequate cooling. Soon the company failed and was converted into a sugar factory.

The year 1838 brought the opening of the oldest, still operating altbier brewpub in Düsseldorf, the Brauerei Ferdinand Schumacher. Its founder, Mathias Schumacher, took the traditional Rhineland ale as he found it, but added a bit more hops than was customary at the time, brewed it stronger, and started to experiment with aging the beer in wooden casks to let it mature. In Schumacher's innovations lie the roots of the modern altbier style: a robust, coppery, slow-fermented, lagered ale. By 1871, Schumacher's operation, then under his son Ferdinand's management, had outgrown its original facilities. A new brewery was built at 123 Oststraße, where, happily for the modern connoisseur, the same alt is still brewed and served today.

The schloßturm (castle tower) is the only structure still standing from Johann Wilhelm's residence. The drawing above dates from the beginning; the photo below, from the end of the twentieth century.

By the end of the nineteenth century, several scientific and technological developments posed both a new threat to the ale houses of the Rhineland and an opportunity for significant quality improvements. Yeast was not discovered until 1674, more than one-and-a-half centuries after the original Bavarian beer-purity law. We owe this giant leap to Antony van Leeuwenhoek, a Dutch spectacle-maker and the inventor of the first useable microscope. Van Leeuwenhoek was also the first to see bacteria and other protozoans (single-cell organisms) as well as red blood cells.

It took another one-and-a-half centuries or so, until 1837, before scientists figured out that yeast is a living organism that metabolizes (ferments) sugars. That credit goes to Theodor Schwann, a German physiologist and histologist, who called yeast a "sugar fungus," or *Saccharomyces* in Latin. This set the stage for the Danish botanist Emil Christian Hansen, who, in 1881, classified Schwann's sugar fungus into cold, bottom-fermenting, lager strains (*Saccharomyces uvarum*) and warm, top-fermenting, ale strains (*Saccharomyces cerevisiae*). Since Hansen, all other yeasts (which produce nasty off-flavors in beer) are called "wild." *Saccharomyces uvarum*, incidentally, is also known as *Saccharomyces carlsbergensis* after Hansen's employer, the Carlsberg Brewing Company of Copenhagen.

Hansen further noted that, within the two broad classes of beer-friendly top- and bottom-fermenting yeasts, there are many variations, each with their own properties that affect the ultimate taste of the beer they ferment. By 1890, he had developed a practical technique for the cultivation of pure yeast strains from a single cell. Pitching was no longer a matter of chance.

By the middle of the nineteenth century, it was also clearly understood that different yeasts work best only within their own, very narrow temperature ranges. But until the invention of mechanical refrigeration by the German engineer Carl von Linde, in 1873, brewers had to use blocks of ice harvested during the winter and stored in ice houses to regulate the temperature of their fermentation cellars. Von Linde called his first working model of the refrigerator an ammonia cold machine. It was based on the principle that a compressed gas absorbs heat from its surroundings when it is permitted to expand. He used an electric motor to compress gaseous ammonia into a liquid. He then released it into the coils of a refrigeration compartment. There the ammonia reverted to its gaseous form and, in the process, drew heat from its environment. Then the motor repeated the cycle by converting the ammonia gas back into a liquid, and so on. To this day, the compressors and evaporators in a modern brewery, though now operating with other refrigerants such as freon or glycol, work according to the same principles that von Linde used in his first cold machine.

Hansen's and von Linde's pioneering work, which occurred only a little more than a hundred years ago, made the modern lager revolution possible. Brewers certainly had made lager beers before then. But, because fermentation was usually carried out in open fermenters by inevitably mixed yeast cultures and—without refrigeration—at relatively high temperatures, the default beer made by most of our predecessors had usually been an ale. Thanks to science and technology, however, by the end of the nineteenth century, brewers were able to make both ales and lagers of predictable quality anywhere they chose.

Within a scant two decades from von Linde's invention of refrigeration, the conversion of German breweries from top fermentation to bottom fermentation was complete—except in the Rhineland. But even there, the commercial production of modern alt and kölsch ales is plainly unthinkable without the use of pure, laboratory-managed, bacteria-free *Saccharomyces cerevisiae* or without rigid temperature control of the mash and the fermenting wort.

Advances in technology, especially steam generation and refrigeration, also made brewing more capital-intensive, and many small breweries folded or were taken over as industrialization, with its large-scale factory breweries, arrived in the nineteenth century. Large breweries also could expand their markets beyond the local horizon as the railway quickly replaced the horse-drawn dray for beer transport.

In Düsseldorf, there were still about 100, mostly small, alt breweries in 1860. By the end of the First World War, only about half of them remained, and of those, fewer than half were small craft brewpubs. By the end of the Second World War, only eighteen breweries survived in Düsseldorf and of those, only three large ones and four brewpubs have weathered the mergers of the past few decades.

Credit is due to the Rhineland for preserving the 3,000-year-old German ale heritage as a still-vibrant expression of the country's beer culture at a time when the global lager revolution turned most of the "old" brews into "beerological" fossils. Today, Düsseldorf is a thoroughly forward-looking, modern city; the capital of North-Rhine-Westphalia; a renowned center of fashion and finance; and still the home of Germany's traditional beer, the alt—that rich, mellow brew of unsurpassed elegance and ancient lineage.

CHAPTER 2

Altbier
Profile

The city center of Düsseldorf is called the *altstadt* ("old town"). Many of the buildings in the altstadt date from the thirteenth to the seventeenth centuries. Though the altstadt was not named for the altbier nor vice versa, the verbal association between the two is both fortuitous and appropriate. In the Rhineland, the altstadt is known affectionately as the longest bar in the world, as almost every building within a square mile contains a pub serving alt—there are about 200 of them. If you ask for a beer in Düsseldorf, you get an alt. If you want a Pils or a weizen, you have to ask for it specifically. In the altstadt you find three of the four altbier brewpubs that have defined the style for our age. These are the Uerige, Im Füchschen, and Zum Schlüssel. The fourth is called Schumacher. It is located at 123 Oststraße, about a mile east of the altstadt.

Though named Altstadt Alt, this beer is not made in Düsseldorf but in Bochum, some 35 miles to the northeast.

These brewpubs are cozy, modestly priced places with friendly, down-to-earth service. There you can absorb the local atmosphere and enjoy the joviality of the Rhenish people. Long, scrubbed-down, wooden tables surrounded by wooden benches give these  pubs their rustic feel. In some of the niches and recesses of the Uerige pub, old hectoliter-size wooden beer casks are given a new purpose by serving as center tables for rounds of happy imbibers. Düsseldorf's brew-pubs offer a hearty fare. The dishes they serve include pickled herring on rye bread, pig's knuckle with sauerkraut, bratwurst with potato salad, rolls with aged cheese or blood sausage, raw onion rings, and a hot local mustard—all washed down with copious quantities of alt.

Alt is a sublime taste and texture experience. It is always difficult to express in words what we perceive by seeing, hearing, tasting, or smelling. Just as the poet cannot replace the painter, the scribe cannot do justice to the brewer's gustatory art. Words convey emotions and facts indirectly, whereas the senses grasp our world immediately. Thus, any description of the sensory characteristics of a beer style is, by necessity, somewhat subjective and always inade-quate. If you have access to an authentic, fresh alt, use the beer itself rather than this chapter as your sensory yardstick. If you have never tasted a real alt, perhaps the following lines will convey, however imperfectly, what the alt style is all about.

If alt were a British beer, it would rank on the flavor spectrum somewhere between a brown and a dark ale. As a German brew, however, alt has a few distinctly continental characteristics. Because of the way altbier is mashed, it is generally fuller-bodied than a typical British ale. All altbiers are multistep-mashed, by partial decoction, by infusion, or by a combination of the two methods. An alt grain bed must be taken through all three temperature ranges required to  activate the three crucial enzymes in brewing: proteolytic enzymes, beta-amylase, and alpha-amylase.

Proteolytic enzymes convert large, heavy grain proteins into smaller, lighter ones. Beta-amylase convert grain starches into simple, fermentable sugars such as maltose. Alpha-amylase convert grain starches into complex, unfermentable sugars such as dextrins. Although brewers yeast turns simple sugars

A proper alt should be served in a straight-sided 0.2-, 0.3-, or 0.4- liter glass.

(produced by beta-amylase) into alcohol, it cannot break down proteins and dextrins. These stay in the finished alt. They are completely tasteless to humans. Texture, not flavor or alcoholic strength, is their most important function. They add body and mouthfeel to brews that might otherwise be perceived as too thin and weak.

Proteins and dextrins also form an invisible web in the alt, through which carbon dioxide bubbles must work their way slowly to the surface. As a result, full-bodied beer remains effervescent longer. Its bubbles remain smaller and do not combine into large pockets of burpy gas, as happens in carbonated mineral water, for instance. Once carbon dioxide bubbles reach the surface, they drag part of the invisible web out of the brew, where the proteins and dextrins form a rich, creamy, long-lasting head, one of the defining characteristics of an alt as opposed to a British ale.

A pronounced, almost slightly sweet malt flavor complements the rich texture of the alt. The alt's maltiness has no roasty overtones. It balances the beer's moderate up-front bitterness and noble hop finish. The result is a bittersweet to nutty brew with a lingering but never cloying aftertaste.

Crispness is another aspect that distinguishes an alt from a British ale. This cleanliness of palate comes from the practice—unusual for ale brewers—of cool fermenting and lagering the alt. True lagering (from the German word *lagern,* meaning "to store") involves the aging and maturing of the beer *on the yeast* near the freezing point.

Alts generally stay in the fermenter at least twice as long as do British ales, and invariably at lower temperatures. The lower the fermentation temperature, the slower is the beer's fermentation and the smaller is the amount of off-flavors released by the yeast. These off-flavors come mostly from estery fermentation by-products. Prolonged lagering allows the yeast to re-absorb, through its cell membrane, many of these unpleasant-tasting by-products of its own metabolism. In a sense, the yeast "cleans" the beer, which is the true wonder of beer maturation through lagering. Long periods of cold maturation also allow any remaining sulfur dioxide (SO_2), which is a natural by-product of the yeast's fermentation, to become volatile and escape from the beer. An alt that has been lagered for about four to six weeks, therefore, becomes clean, soft, and mellow.

German altbiers are made not only in and around Düsseldorf, but also outside the Rhineland in such cities as Oelde, Münster, and Steinfurt in Westphalia; Frankfurt in Hesse; Hanover and Brunswick in Lower

Saxony; and even Großostheim, a small village near Aschaffenburg in Bavaria. These non-Rhenish alts, though, have been historically less significant for setting the style. Most of these altbiers are similar to the Düsseldorf model, with southern alts being a bit sweeter and maltier, Hanoverian alts being slightly darker, and Münster alts being a bit more sour because of the addition of a substantial amount of wheat to the grain bill.

The larger of the Düsseldorf alt breweries are now owned by national and international beverage conglomerates that distribute their products all over Germany, while the smaller breweries are generally still family-owned and distribute their beers in local markets only. The alt is one of about a dozen major beer styles in Germany. For decades, its market share has hovered around 3–4%. This is roughly the same sales volume as that for its ale cousin, the kölsch, from neighboring Cologne. The Pilsener, by comparison, which is Germany's most popular beer style, holds a market share almost twenty times that large.

In North America, the alt is still a very rare bird. The German originals are generally not imported, and the few examples of the style made by North American craftbreweries are generally not widely or reliably distributed. Thus, if you live in the New World and want to taste an authentic alt, you probably have to brew it yourself or travel to

Germany, specifically to the Rhineland. Appendix A contains a select list of commercial altbiers from Germany and North America.

CHAPTER 3

Altbier
Ingredients

To make an authentic German alt, at home or in a craftbrewery, you must choose the grains, water, hops, and yeast strains that are characteristic of the style. Then you must combine these in the right quantities—using appropriate mash-tun, kettle, and cellar processes—to develop the correct flavor, color, and texture.

In this chapter, we look at some of the variables that are important in the selection of altbier ingredients. Where necessary, we touch briefly on the underlying chemistry, microbiology, or other technical factors that make one ingredient more suitable than another. However, in general, we focus on the practical questions that brewers encounter rather than on the science behind these variables.

The grain specs for altbier are relatively broad and allow the brewer a fairly large degree of freedom. You can compose your grain bill from light malts, moderately dark malts, or a combination of the two—as long as you avoid overly toasty varieties. You can make your alt with imported or North American malts. As a general rule, though, if you have a choice, you probably want to avoid grain from suppliers that emphasize the suitability of their products for British-style ales, as these grains tend to be lower in protein and produce wort with less body than is desirable for an authentic alt. Just for the record, all batches described in chapter 6 were made with grains from the Briess Malting Company. Suitable extract brands are, among others, Ireks, BierKeller, and Laaglander.

You can brew an authentic alt from both hard and soft water—as long as you know how to correct your mash pH (in most places in North America you probably have to lower it) and adjust your hop loading accordingly.

In the selection of hop varieties, the altbier brewer has comparatively fewer choices. To achieve the correct alt flavor involves more than just plugging a theoretical IBU target into a mathematical formula and then weighing out the required amount of any old hops. Alt hops should not be too fruity or too assertive. German noble hops—though sometimes fairly expensive—or their North American–grown equivalents give by far the best results. Hops are not the place to save money when it comes to brewing a quality altbier! Also note that otherwise wonderful aroma hops such as the English East Kent Golding and Fuggle or the ubiquitous North American Cascade are singularly unsuitable for brewing altbier.

Yeast is arguably *the* defining variable in the formulation of altbier. Alt yeasts are true strains of *Saccharomyces cerevisiae*; that is, of ale yeast. They are sometimes, however, incorrectly referred to as hybrids, because their metabolic performance places them somewhere in the middle between typical British ale yeasts and typical German lager yeasts.

From these broad guidelines it follows that there is no need for dogmatism in the discussion of altbier making—except when it comes to the choice of yeast! Other important guidelines for formulating your altbiers include the desirability of so-called noble hops varieties and the avoidance of overly roasty components in your grain bill. Probably the most important factor in making an alt is the brewer's understanding of the beer style itself. Then the brewer must figure out how the brewing process turns the materials at hand into the target style. It is the authenticity of the result that counts, and the roads to the same destination are many.

Grain

Authentic altbiers are made mostly from light Pils malt (*helles malz*), Vienna malt (*Wiener malz*), and Munich malt (dark, *dunkel, Münchener malz*). Higher-Lovibond malts such as caramel and crystal (*farbmalz*) or chocolate and black (*röstmalz*) are used only sparingly, if at all.

The work horse of altbier brewing, as in fact of German brewing in general, is what is variously called  pale, light, blonde, or Pils malt (*helles malz*). It is made from two-row summer barley. Summer grains tend to have higher protein levels than do winter grains. During malting, the barley for Pils malt is allowed to germinate at or slightly below room temperature for up to seven days. It is then dried gently for one to three days. The result of this rather slow drying cycle is a malt that is considered fairly pale by North American standards, but is excellently suited as the foundation malt of a German lagered ale such as the alt. For a more detailed description of German malting techniques, see appendix B.

German *helles* Pils malt has a color rating of about 1–1.5 °L. North American two-row malts of up to 2 °L are perfectly acceptable as a foundation grist for altbier, provided their protein level is around 12% or more. Continental European barley has always been comparatively higher in proteins than, for instance, the barley varieties grown in the maritime climate of the British Isles or in much of North America. Proteins in barley, when properly degraded ("modified") during malting and mashing, contribute body and mouthfeel to beer and account for the creamy, long-lasting head so characteristic of many authentic German brews. Six-row barley, the standard foundation grain of North American adjunct-laden, mass-produced beers, is never used in alt brewing. Six-row barley can impart a slightly rough, grainy flavor to the fermented beer that would run counter to the smooth, mellow finish you should expect from a properly made alt.

When brewing with extract as the base for your alt, always choose the palest of the pale lager malts available from your supplier. Remember, you can always darken your wort by the addition of higher-Lovibond malts, but you can never remove wort color once it is there. Always buy a lager malt, even though the alt is an ale! If you have a choice, select a can of extract recommended for such German lagers as Pils, Pilsener, helles, or Dortmunder instead of British pale ales. For an optimum match of grain varieties, it is preferable to purchase an extract malt imported from Germany or one of its neighboring countries where full-bodied beers are the norm. For best results, buy cans of unhopped malt and add your own hops to the kettle rather than rely on the—usually unspecified and probably not appropriate—hops chosen by the extract manufacturer.

Vienna malts (Wiener malz) are a shade darker than Pils malts. They are often part of an alt grain bill. Made from the same barley as Pils malts, they undergo longer kilning at slightly higher temperatures. The result is a slightly amber but not roasted malt, ideally suited to add darker notes to an alt. German Vienna malt has a color rating of approximately 2–3 °L, while the rating for North American Vienna malt is usually 1 °L higher.

Munich malts (dark, dunkel, Münchener malz) are darker yet and often contribute a slight sweetness, in addition to color, to the alt. They are dried even longer and at a higher temperature. The result is a *slightly* roasted, but never burned, grain. In many alts, the coppery color stems from Munich malts with a color rating of about 8–12 °L.

When making alt from extract, it always improves the authenticity of your brew if you steep a certain amount of Vienna and Munich malts in your brewing liquor before adding the canned lager malt.

The true color malts—caramel, crystal, chocolate, and black—are usually from lightly to severely roasted or even burned. Their use is common in dark, British-style ales such as stouts and porters, but they are used only extremely sparingly or not at all in altbiers. Whereas dark, British-style ales—also brewed from a foundation of pale malt—require plenty of highly kilned malts to achieve their opaque appearance and sometimes coffeelike taste, German ales get most of their color from a greater addition of Munich and Vienna malts.

No matter whether you brew from grain or from extract, experiment with different brands of caramel or crystal malts. It is possible to compose an authentic, all-grain alt with 15–20% color malts at a Lovibond rating of 60° and still make an alt. Likewise, you can make an authentically tasting extract alt by steeping some color malt in your brewing liquor. The key variable is how the maltster achieved the grain's dark color: quickly at a higher temperature or slowly at a lower temperature. Always remember, if you can taste roasted notes in your brew, it is not an authentic alt, even if the color is a perfect, deep copper.

Water

Brewing water should be low in or void of organic contaminants. If your water source is high in contaminants, consider installing an activated carbon filter. If maintained according to the manufacturer's instructions, such filters can very effectively improve the

taste, smell, and appearance of your water and the beer you make from it. Carbon filters, however, do not trap minerals responsible for water hardness, nor do they eliminate nitrate pollutants often associated with agricultural runoff.

Water hardness or softness, which is the level of dissolved mineral ions, and the related pH-value are the other crucial water variables that can influence your beer's characteristics. As a simple rule for interpreting a water analysis report, "harder" water gives you a more alkaline mash (increases your mash pH), whereas "softer" water gives you a more acidic mash (lowers your mash pH).

The numerical relationship between water hardness and softness, on the one hand, and the pH value of your mash, on the other hand, is very complex and confusing. Suffice it to say that, as a home- or craftbrewer, you should always have strips of pH test paper in your arsenal and take a reading every time you mash in. For a more technical treatise of the relationship between mash pH and water hardness, consult appendix C.

If your mash is too alkaline, you can easily correct the problem by adding a bit of gypsum (calcium sulfate) to your brewing liquor. It takes about 15 grams (roughly 1 teaspoon) of gypsum in a 5-gallon batch to lower your mash pH by the equivalent of about 250 parts per million (ppm). If your mash turns out to be too acidic, which is not very likely in North America, your best choice is to work with paler malts, as there is a direct relationship between mash acidity and grain color, or to add a smidgen of chalk (calcium carbonate) *to the mash*, not to the brewing water. The optimum mash pH value for an alt is between 5 and 5.8. Commercial alt breweries that avoid color malts tend to work with a mash pH of 5.5–5.7, while those that do add color malts tend to have a mash pH of about 5. A good target for the North American home- or craft-brewer is a value of pH 5.4.

In greater Düsseldorf, today's altbier is made mostly with city water, which has an average hardness of 215–235 ppm (expressed in ppm of $CaCO_3$, which is calcium carbonate). In the inner city, water hardness is usually about 270 ppm. Compare these values from Düsseldorf with the hardness values of your own water as furnished by your local water works or by a private water analysis lab. Some alt breweries in Düsseldorf treat (soften) their water with calcium hydroxide [$Ca(OH)_2$], also known as slaked lime, which causes both calcium and bicarbonates to precipitate. This lowers the mash pH. Other breweries, including some of the top brewpubs in the city, take their brewing liquor as is, straight from the faucet.

For comparison, the following is a list of water hardness values for a few famous European brewing centers (in ppm calcium carbonate), ranked from soft to hard water:

Pilsen	30
London	235
Munich	250
Dublin	300
Vienna	750
Dortmund	750
Burton	875

Altbier brewing, however, is not restricted to Düsseldorf. Fine alts are brewed in Westphalia, Lower Saxony, Hesse, and even Bavaria. Because the German beer-purity law (Reinheitsgebot) allows for the treatment of brewing liquor, you can brew any style of beer, including an alt, anywhere in Germany regardless of the local water characteristics.

Luckily for the North American brewer, most of the groundwater available in the central portion of the continent is suitable for altbier brewing without modification. The closer you live near either the Atlantic or the Pacific coast, however, the softer your water becomes. Altbier brewing liquor should be medium hard, roughly on a par with the waters of such famous brewing cities as Munich, London, and Dublin. If you have formulated your grain bill correctly and your mash pH is too high for an authentic alt (i.e., it exceeds 5.8), either correct your brewing liquor for excessive alkalinity or increase the color value of your grain bed.

Because alt breweries in Germany make fine beers across the board, we can conclude that it is possible to make authentic alts with a relatively large variation in water hardness. The brewing process employed in alt making and the characteristics of the grains, hops, and yeast used in the process appear to have a much greater effect on the end result than does the composition of the water.

Hops

The critical hop variables for an authentic alt, as for any beer, are the hop's bittering capability and its general flavor and aroma profile. Hops additions to the wort are generally labeled bittering, flavor, and aroma, causing some authors to use the terms *flavor* and *aroma* interchangeably. For the purpose of altbier making (and German beermaking in general), we should use these terms in a narrower context. Bittering, flavor, and aroma are contributed to the beer by different compounds in the hops, each with different levels of wort solubility and heat-sensitive volatility. Bittering hops are therefore added at or shortly after the beginning of the boil. Flavor hops are

added at or near the end of the boil, and aroma hops are added after the boil.

The bittering in beer stems mostly from the hop's alpha acids (humulones, cohumulones, adhumulones). These soft resins are relatively stable compounds, as long as the hops are stored cold. Alpha acids oxidize over time, at which point they can no longer contribute to the wort's bitterness. Unoxidized alpha acids become soluble in wort only after prolonged exposure to intense heat. This process is called isomerization and involves the rearrangement of the molecule's atoms into iso-alpha-acids during the kettle boil.

Beta acids are another group of soft resins that contribute marginally to wort bitterness. Called lupulones, colupulones, and adlupulones, these beta acids are about as stable as alpha acids but are less wort-soluble, unless they are oxidized. Over time, beta acids oxidize into hulupones, particularly in European noble hops varieties. If you use aged hops, hulupones can supply up to 50% of the hops' bitterness and are thus added deliberately to certain beers—but not alt—to compensate for any loss in alpha-acid bitterness from old hops. For all practical purposes, therefore, we can ignore the role of beta acids in altbier making, provided the bittering hops you use are fresh.

Hop flavor is mostly based on the oxidation products and other compounds derived from volatile hop oils. These are hydrocarbons. Most influential among them are myrcene, humulene, caryophyllene, and farnesene. Especially myrcene escapes quickly or oxidizes under exposure to heat. Some of their derivatives survive best in a short, but not in a prolonged, rolling boil in the kettle. Hop flavor, therefore, comes primarily from the hops that is added to the wort near or at the end of the boil.

Hop aroma also stems from the hops' volatile, essential oils and their derivatives, but stays in the beer only if not exposed to high heat for any length of time. Hop aroma thus comes from hops added after the boil, when the temperature of the wort starts to drop or even when the wort is cool.

The astringent component of the hop flavor spectrum comes mostly from polyphenols, such as tannins. These are soluble in wort, but a large portion of them adheres to coagulating proteins and precipitates out into the trub.

For altbier, then, we need bittering hops that are fairly neutral in character and fresh. Avoid bittering varieties that are known to impart acrid, pungent, spicy, floral, citrus, or piney notes to beer. Also avoid old, oxidized bittering hops. These flavors would interfere with the herbal profile generally characteristic of central European noble hops varieties.

The basic principle for hopping altbiers is *noblésse oblige*. The lower the cohumulone (an alpha acid) content and the higher the humulene (an aroma oil) content of the hops, the "nobler" is its lineage. Typical German noble hops varieties suitable for alt are Hallertau, Tettnanger, Perle, or Spalt. Unlike many British ales or northern German lagers, most (but not all) alts tend to have less pronounced bittering notes. Instead, malty components dominate as does hop aroma.

Most German alt brewers use two kettle additions of hops. The first addition occurs early in the boil (for bittering); the second occurs toward the middle or end of the boil (for flavor). Some brewers use the same variety, such as Hallertau Mittelfrüh, for both bittering and flavor, whereas others prefer different varieties, such as Perle and Spalt, for the two additions. Some use one addition each of the same hops at the beginning and the end of the boil (for bittering and flavor) and a second hops variety for beer aroma during a third addition as the wort cools off, usually in the whirlpool. Only a few alt brewers dry hop their wort in the tank to accentuate aroma.

A good North American bittering and flavor hop for alt is Mt. Hood (a triploid variety bred from Hallertau

Mittelfrüh), while North American Tettnanger is well suited as an aroma hop. Note that the North American–grown Hallertau hop is not a good substitute for German Hallertau, in spite of its name and its biological origin as a transplanted Hallertau Mittelfrüh.

In Germany, as in North America, pellets are gaining in appeal, but several alt brewers insist on using only leaf hops. Tradition is one reason for this preference, the higher amount of tannins in leaf hops is another, since tannins aid in the coagulation of excess wort protein in the kettle and thus improve beer clarity and stability. These brewers point out, however, that it is essential to use only fresh leaf hops (from

Copper altbier brew kettle.

the current harvest year) that have been cold stored at 32–37 °F (0–3 °C) to prevent unacceptable losses in hop quality.

Yeast

The best altbier—as the best beer in general—is, of course, made with pure and healthy yeast strains. Although most beer styles can be made with any number of yeast strains, this is not the case with alt. Because of the particular fermentation regimen employed in authentic altbier making, relatively few strains perform to style.

Yeast suitable for altbier making belong to the category of *Saccharomyces cerevisiae* (top-fermenting ale yeast) as opposed to *Saccharomyces uvarum* (bottom-fermenting lager yeast). Typical ale yeasts like a cozy, warm environment, somewhere around 59–77 °F (15–25 °C), in which they become most active and produce the best-tasting beer, while typical lager yeasts do their best work when it is a frigid 46–56 °F (8–13 °C) or even below. Ale yeasts go dormant at low temperatures, whereas lager yeasts can still ferment wort.

Both ale and lager yeasts are in suspension throughout the wort, while they metabolize (that is, ferment) sugars and produce alcohol, carbon dioxide, and other substances. Thus the terms *top* and *bottom fermentation* are, strictly speaking, misnomers. The terms refer to the fact that most ale yeasts throw up a thick, frothy, rocky layer of foam at the top of the brew during the vigorous stage of primary fermentation, while most lager yeasts tend to be much less exuberant surface fermenters, developing little or no head at all. Be prepared, therefore, to use a blowoff tube or allow for plenty of head space in your alt fermenter (about 33%). A 5-gallon batch, for instance, is best started in a 6-gallon carboy.

At the end of fermentation, ale yeasts tend to float to the surface more so than do lager yeasts, yet ultimately, both types flocculate and sink to the bottom of the fermenter. Traditionally, alt yeasts were harvested for repitching into the next batch by skimming the foam off the top of the wort in an open fermenter during primary fermentation. In alt breweries with cylindroconical fermenters, yeast is now drawn off the tank bottom for repitching at the end of fermentation.

In both the lager and the ale category, there are well and poorly flocculating yeast strains. Alt yeast strains tend to be poor flocculators, which is why altbier usually benefits from filtration—if you are in a hurry to drink it—or from a long period of lagering in a conditioning tank—if you can wait for nature and gravity to take their course.

While the distinction between top- and bottom-fermenting yeasts may be somewhat spurious, the distinction between warm and cold fermentation is not. If a typical lager yeast is employed at too high a temperature, attenuation will be rapid, but accompanied by an excessive production of esters and other metabolic trace elements that impart unlagerlike, even unpleasant, flavors to the finished beer. Likewise, if a typical ale yeast is employed at too low a temperature, attenuation will be slow and may even get stuck, leaving you with a raw or cloyingly sweet beer that is a poor representative of its style. For additional information

At high kräusen, alt yeast produces a thick, rocky layer of foam. During fermentation in open vats, the yeast is skimmed off into buckets for repitching.

about the biology of brewers yeast and its taxonomic classification, see appendix D.

Here comes the contradiction: Alt yeasts, though true ale yeasts, are not typical. They are neither warm nor cold fermenters. As there is no specific term for such yeasts in the standard brewing literature (except for the misleading term *hybrids*, which they are not), let's call alt yeasts "cool" fermenters. During primary fermentation, they do their best work at a cool—but not cold—temperature of roughly 55–66 °F (13–19 °C). The cleanest-tasting results are achieved if primary fermentation is carried out at the lower end of this temperature range. Alt yeast becomes dormant at a temperature of about 45 °F (7 °C).

It is for reasons of temperature tolerance that you must use a true alt yeast if you want to make an authentic altbier. All the batches described in chapter 6 were made with WYEAST 1007, which is convenient to use because it comes with its own starter solution in a sterile pouch. But there are also several other sources, some local, some countrywide, of German-style ale yeasts suitable for altbier making. Inquire at your supplier.

All alt yeasts available to the North American home- or craftbrewer seem to come in liquid form only. There appear to be no dried alt yeasts on the market. If you start your alt with a Pils malt extract kit that comes with a packet of dried yeast, *do not use this yeast!* Alt yeasts are specialists: They make nothing but altbier, and altbier cannot be made from anything but alt yeast. Treat this rule like a commandment. It's nonnegotiable!

CHAPTER 4

Altbier Equipment for the Homebrewer

Let's first look at a typical, real-life, commercial altbier system used in Germany so that we know what we have to imitate when we design our homebrew equipment in the North American context.

In Germany, a commercial craftbrew system usually consists of a two-vessel arrangement: a combination mash tun/brew kettle and a separate lauter tun. Breweries that still employ a traditional decoction mash also have a separate cooker. The mash/brew kettle is steam-heated to take the grain bed through its temperature steps. The mash is then pumped to the lauter tun with the false bottom for sparging. Next, the grain residue is rinsed out of the kettle, so the kettle can receive the runoff from the lauter tun for boiling and hopping. Before heat-exchanging, the hot wort is often filtered or centrifuged in Germany.

In the cellar, alt is often passed through three to five separate tanks: a primary fermenter (usually a conical unitank or, in more traditional setups, a flat open vat); one or two secondary fermenters; a lagering tank, where the alt is allowed to mature on the yeast; and a conditioning tank into which the beer is filtered and often blended for consistency.

Transferring alt in Düsseldorf.

After lagering, the mature altbier is usually sent through a two-stage filter. The filter medium at the first stage is usually diatomaceous earth, and the medium at the second stage is a set of sheets often made from cellulose. After filtration, the clear beer is held in conditioning tanks before bottling and kegging.

In North America, craft-breweries often combine the mash tun with the lauter tun and have a separate, often direct-fired brew kettle. Instead of a wort filter, microbreweries often use a separate vessel as a whirlpool or they whirlpool the boiled wort directly in the brew kettle by racking it off the trub and reintroducing it through a tangential arm back into the kettle. A mash/lauter tun is perfectly suitable for step mashing authentic altbier; however, a good mash-tun agitator with a powerful motor for slow revolutions (about 1/2–1 revolutions per minute) as well as steam-jacketed walls make the task much more manageable.

Many mash/lauter tuns available to the craftbrew industry are not well suited for alt making. Because an authentic alt, like a true German lager, requires a step-mashing process, the mash tun must be capable of heating up the grain bed from one temperature range to the next. A steam-jacketed, insulated, stainless-steel mash tun is the most functional equipment for this purpose. The jackets should envelop both the bottom and the wall of the mash tun, whereby the wall jackets should be at least as high as the top level of the grain bed. At the start of a step mash in a commercial mash/lauter tun, it is best to dough in (create a thick mash) for the protein rest at the first temperature level and then to raise the temperature for the sugar rest by infusing the mash with hot water while steam-heating the mash tun. A good, slow-moving mash agitator (or a great deal of brawn) are needed to stir the mash while it is being heated. This prevents hot spots in the grain bed that would destroy enzymes.

If your mash tun is designed for British-style, single-step infusions only, you must rely entirely on hot-water infusions to raise your temperature between the different mash steps. In this case, make sure that you choose a grain volume that leaves sufficient room for the addition of hot water without causing the mash tun to overflow. In such a system you will probably also have to reach your mash-out temperature *through* sparging rather than *before* sparging.

At home, too, in order to make a proper altbier from all grain, you need the ability to step-infusion mash. You must imitate the commercial process, but almost certainly without the benefit of a steam-jacketed mash tun. In the homebrew setup proposed here, the mash tun is separate from the lauter tun, as is the case in a typical German system, simply because it is too complicated to make a multistep mash/lauter tun for use in the home.

With a little bit of ingenuity, you can make your own alt brew house from parts available at your kitchen supply store and your hardware store. As with all homebrewing from grain, you need a grain mill, available from your homebrew supply store, and a kitchen scale (preferably with a range of up to 20 pounds or 10 kilograms). The only item that may be difficult to find is a proper recirculation pump. But once assembled, your Lilliputian altbier brew house can also be used to make authentic lagers.

Home Mash Tun

For a mash tun, use a 5- to 7-gallon stock pot or a similar vessel. Old milk cans that are sometimes available at farm auctions also work well. As in a German system, the mash tun also doubles as brew kettle. After you have step mashed your grain, raise the temperature to the mash-out level and use a pitcher or measuring cup to transfer the grain into the lauter tun.

A modified 5-gallon stock pot serves as a home lautering tun.

Home Lauter Tun with Recirculation

To make a lauter tun, you need a second 5- to 7-gallon stock pot and a colander. Because of the modifications you have to make to them, they should both be made from stainless steel rather than enamel-coated metal. Because the colander serves as a false lauter bottom, its upper rim width must be close to the inside diameter of the stock pot. If the colander handles are in the way, cut them off with a hacksaw. The colander should stand on solid legs, perhaps 1/2 to 1 inch high, around which liquid can flow freely. If the colander is supported by an inverted, cup-shaped hollow that can trap liquids, cut it off at the tack welds with a hacksaw. To make new legs for the colander, drill three to five holes into its bottom through which you fasten bolts with lock washers and nuts. The long ends of the bolts point down. They serve as legs that hold the colander above the stock-pot bottom and allow wort to drain without obstruction.

If there is a small gap between the rim of the colander and the inside wall of the stock pot, you need to create a good seal between the two. Cut a piece of plastic tubing the length of the circumference of the colander. Splice it open lengthwise and slide it around the colander rim. If there is still too much of a gap, cut a second tube the length of the inner circumference of the stock pot. Fill this tube with sand or air-rifle pellets and turn it into a ring by sliding the two ends over an inch or two of smaller-diameter tubing. Use two hose clamps to hold the joined tube ends firmly in place on the inner connecting piece to prevent liquid from entering the tube ring. Place this heavy plastic-tube ring inside the stock pot on top of the colander rim with the first tube. You should now have a tight seal between the false bottom (colander) and the mash-tun wall (stock pot). The sand or pellets keep the ring from becoming buoyant once the mash tun is filled with grain and water.

A stainless-steel colander serves as a false mash bottom. Rings made from plastic tubing seal the false bottom against the mash-tun wall.

Depending on the size and spacing of the holes in the colander, it is often advisable to line the colander with one or more layers of cheesecloth to keep grain particles from being flushed into the wort and obstructing the wort passages. Let the cheesecloth overlap the colander rim. You can use the spliced plastic tubing to crimp the cheesecloth in place. Use fresh cheesecloth for every mash.

To prepare the stock pot for lautering, drill a hole in one side of the pot about half an inch from the bottom. Feed about 2 inches of threaded copper pipe through the pot wall and fasten the pipe to the pot wall, on the inside and the outside, with two rubber-gasketed retaining nuts. Equal lengths of the threaded copper pipe should stick into and out of the pot. Screw a copper elbow to the inside end of the copper pipe. Let the elbow point down. This is your racking arm. At the other end, thread a ball valve to the copper pipe. Connect some plastic tubing to the outflow of the ball valve. This leads to the input side of a small pump, which serves as a recirculation and wort transfer pump. Connect the pump input port to the plastic tubing. For the output side of the pump, use plastic tubing and several copper reducers, if need be, to connect to a piece of quarter-inch-diameter copper pipe bent to lead the pumped wort back to the top of the grain bed. Drill two holes in the lid of the stock pot, one for the copper pipe from the pump, the other for a thermometer (get a good, water-tight thermometer). This completes your lauter tun's recirculation plumbing.

Once the wort runs clear, move the quarter-inch-diameter copper pipe to the brew kettle and use the pump to transfer the wort to the kettle. Let the tip of the pipe rest near the bottom of the kettle to avoid hot-side aeration from splashing wort.

Finding the right pump might take some doing. Stainless-steel pumps are usually prohibitively expensive, and pumps made from other materials may not be suitable. Pumps must be made of material that is of food-grade quality and rated for high

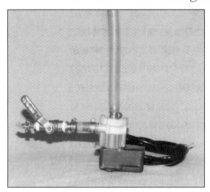

temperatures. Suitable non-stainless-steel, food-grade pumps are likely to be rated for 190 °F (88 °C). Avoid pumps with exposed bearings that could leak grease into the wort.

One such pump that works well was originally designed to recirculate water from a holding tank for live lobsters. This pump is very sturdy, as it is designed to run without interruption for years. The impeller and casing are made from inert material that is rated for 190 °F (88 °C), which is surprising because lobsters like it cold! Shop around. Such a pump is likely to be available for slightly below $100 at the distributor. Prices may vary, of course,

Originally intended for a lobster tank, this pump makes a handy wort recirculation pump.

depending on your source and location. If you can't find a pump or do not wish to incur the expense or the trouble, you can use gravity plus a measuring cup or a pitcher to accomplish all tasks performed by the pump. It may take a little longer (especially the heat exchange), but it works just as well.

Home Whirlpool

At the end of the boil and after the final hops addition, stir the wort gently and carefully with a sterile plastic paddle or spoon, but again avoid aeration of hot wort. Do not use a wooden stirrer, because you cannot sterilize wood and the wort may no longer be hot enough to kill bacteria that are likely to reside in the wood. Stirring creates a whirlpool effect that forces the trub (mostly coagulants and hops debris) first to the side of the kettle and then to the bottom. Siphon (rack) hot wort carefully off the trub into your lauter tun—with the colander removed. Make sure the ball valve is closed. Again, be careful not the aerate the hot wort. Whirlpool again to eliminate additional trub.

Home Heat Exchanger

Use the recirculation pump again, but this time to feed your heat exchanger. Simply slip one end of a piece of plastic tubing over the end of your recirculation

Metal-pipe coil serves as a wort chiller.

pipe, and slip the other end over the opening of a 50-foot-long, quarter-inch-diameter copper coil, which serves as a heat exchanger. Use plastic tubing to connect the output end of the copper coil to the lip of your carboy or other primary fermentation vessel. Plug your sink and fill it with cold water. Set the coil inside the sink. Use the pump to force the hot wort through the coil for a heat exchange. Let the cooled wort drip into the carboy or primary fermenter for aeration. Replace the cooling water as often as the wort warms it. For greater efficiency, you can add ice cubes to the water in the sink.

If you do not have a cooling coil, set the wort container into a bucket of ice cubes. Because lukewarm wort is an ideal breeding ground for bacteria, it is important that you reduce the wort temperature quickly, limit the time the wort is exposed to ambient air, and hasten the start of fermentation.

Home Fermentation and Lagering Equipment

For fermenting altbier you need a larger-than-standard primary fermenter, because alt yeast throws up an unusually thick, rocky head of foam. Allow for about 33% head space. For a 5-gallon batch, for instance, use at least a 6-gallon carboy or firmly secure a blowoff tube to the carboy stopper. For proper fermenting and lagering, you also need one or two dedicated refrigerators, depending on how ambitious you are. In a craftbrewery, cool fermenting and cold lagering are accomplished in glycol-jacketed tanks. Typical British pub-style open fermenters with cooling coils usually do not have the capacity to pull the temperature of the beer down enough for real lagering. Most commercial altbier makers today use closed vessels for secondary fermenting and lagering. Many use closed vessels for primary fermenting as well. Closed, jacketed vessels not only isolate the beer from airborne microbes, but they also allow for optimum temperature control over a wide range regardless of the season.

The cellar regimen for altbier, unfortunately, can present a challenge to the homebrewer, especially in regions of the continent with relatively high ambient temperatures for much or all of the year. If you live in a place where nature is not on your side, rigging up an altbier cellar environment for your fermenters and lagering containers can be a space- and energy-intensive proposition.

The average home refrigerator has a temperature range between 40 °F (4 °C) for the coldest setting and 60 °F (16 °C) for the warmest setting. Fortunately, you can make a great alt at a primary fermentation temperature of 60 °F (16 °C), while 40 °F (4 °C) is at the upper limit of the alt lagering temperature. Thus you can use an unmodified refrigerator as your home-brewery cellar for altbier making. But the slickest solution consists of two refrigerators: one for fermenting alt, the other for lagering it.

If you wish to drop your lagering temperature closer to the freezing point, or if you wish to make an authentic German lager beer as well, you need to modify your refrigerators by bypassing their built-in thermostats and replacing them with external thermostats of the appropriate range. *Do not attempt to bypass your refrigerator's thermostat or modify any of its wiring yourself if you are electrically challenged!* If you find your refrigerator's wiring confusing, seek the advice or help of a competent person. Offer a case of your brew in exchange for help. You'd be surprised what people will do for free beer!

Auxiliary thermostats with a wider temperature range than your refrigerator's built-in thermostat are available at many homebrew supply stores, at hardware stores, or from heating and air conditioning suppliers. Usually, such thermostats are connected to your electrical outlet for power and to a probe that must be placed through the door seal inside the refrigerator for temperature monitoring. The refrigerator power cord then plugs into the thermostat. In this setup, the refrigerator's compressor is regulated by the auxiliary temperature probe and thermostat instead of by the refrigerator's own, built-in controls.

Home Filter

Alt yeasts are not very flocculant, and some are downright dusty. If they do not settle out quickly enough for you, you can add finings to your alt after lagering and rack it off the sediment. You can also filter your alt, as do commercial breweries, but for the homebrewer filtering is definitely optional, as filters are not cheap. Expect to spend at least $100 to $200 for a filter. Filter efficiency, or "sharpness," is rated in microns. One micron is one-thousandth of a millimeter.

A home filter is the most elegant solution for beer clarity. Unfortunately, filters are not cheap. A replaceable filter cartridge is usually good for eighty to one hundred 5-gallon batches. Filter sheets can be used only once.

The sharpest filters are called "sterile." They can trap particles and microorganisms as small as half a micron in diameter. Avoid such sterile filters for altbier, as they also strip the fermented brew of

proteins and even some of its color. A good filter rating for altbier is about 3–3.5 microns. At this sharpness, the beer undergoes what is called a "polishing" filtration, which is sufficient to eliminate beer turbidity by trapping all suspended yeast cells and most residual particulate.

CHAPTER 5

Altbier Brewing Methods

A look at the practices of commercial alt makers suggests that there is more than one way of brewing an authentic alt. This chapter discusses in detail the various methods these brewers employ at the different steps of producing their beers, from the choice of their grain for the mash tun to the temperature settings for their lagering tanks. From these guidelines, you can compose your own brewing process tailored to the capabilities of your equipment, the availability of ingredients in your locale, and the preferences of your taste buds. If you wish to follow a more uniform set of guidelines, synthesized from the various practices found in the real world, consult the opening pages of the next chapter.

67

Composing Your Grain Bill

Helles (light, Pils), Vienna, and Munich malts are the foundation grains that give altbiers their body, color, and flavor. Alt brewers tend to regard the higher-Lovibond malts (caramel, crystal, chocolate, and black) strictly as supplemental color malts, not as significant sources of beer flavor.

Most alt brewers in Germany use light Pils malt as the foundation grain. They combine this either with large fractions of Vienna malt, Munich malt, or both or with very small fractions of crystal/caramel or roasted malts added for color. Other alt brewers use about 70% Vienna, 25% Munich, and 5% color malts, and still others use only one type of Pils malt, kilned to a "Munich" color rating of 6 °L, and avoid color malts altogether. There are also alt brewers who use up to 15% color malts as well as 5–15% light wheat malt to round off the flavor. In some alts, the color malt is wheat-based.

Considering these great variations in the grain bills used by the practitioners of German altbier brewing, we should not postulate rigid recipe prescriptions for North American home- and craftbrewers who are trying to become familiar with the style. Instead, choose your grist using the above guidelines while keeping in mind that most breweries that define the alt style use a pale foundation malt with plenty of Vienna and

Munich malts. Compose your own grain bill so the combined color value of your grains produces a coppery ale. Experiment with your grain bill or use the formula in appendix E to guide you.

At the low end of the color scale, the coppery alt may start at 13 °SRM (Standard Research Method, see appendix E). At the high end of the scale, it may have a color rating of 20 °SRM. A few specialty alts are even darker.

When formulating your grain bill, however, be sure to avoid the sharp, toasty overtones that come from too generous a dose of high-Lovibond malts. Consider both color and flavor in your formulation. Some grain bills may yield the mathematically correct color value for alt, but may produce hints of Scotch ale, porter, or stout on the palate, which are completely inappropriate for the style. When in  doubt, err on the side of less crystal, caramel, chocolate, or black malts in favor of more Munich and Vienna malts for color.

It is best to use a well-modified pale foundation malt, because enzymatic strength decreases as malt Lovibond ratings increase. Do not use unmalted, roasted barley or barley flakes, as these add an out-of-style dryness to the beer. Besides, they are a violation of the Rheinheitsgebot.

The maximum, theoretically achievable extract yield for German helles Pils malt, under laboratory conditions, is between 80–82% (dry basis, fine grind) or 78–80% (dry basis, coarse grind) of the solubles contained in the grain, and the difference between the fine and coarse values for the same grain should never exceed two percentage points. The greater the difference between the two extract yields, the smaller is the grain's starch-converting enzymatic strength, and the less suitable is the grain for a pure infusion process. Grains with a low coarse value, therefore, can benefit from at least a partial decoction; that is, the boiling of part of the mash in a separate cooker. The boiling of the grain imitates the starch conversion task usually performed by enzymes in an infusion mash.

In the old days, decoction was often a necessity, because of uncertain grain quality. With easy access to properly malted grains, however, the modern home- and craftbrewer should be able to make a top-quality alt without decoction. Those readers who seek a more in-depth explanation of the decoction process are encouraged to consult Gregory Noonan's *New Brewing Lager Beer* (listed in the references at the end of this book).

The laboratory extract values supplied by malting companies are for comparison only. They can rarely be achieved in a real-life brew house or a homebrew kitchen, where the extract efficiency may be as much as 10–30 percentage points below laboratory values. Several factors account for this discrepancy:

- The maltster's test values are for completely dry grains. The malt you buy still has about 3–4% moisture content, even if it is well kilned. If the grain is stored over long periods of time, it will even re-absorb moisture—originally driven off in the kiln—until it matches the humidity of its environment.

- Grist characteristics achievable in production or home milling are less favorable for extraction than is the perfect grind used for laboratory tests.

- Sparging/lautering of production or home grain beds of varying thicknesses and densities is less efficient than extraction in the laboratory.

- Less than perfect temperature control in the lauter tun can negatively affect extract efficiency, as can lauter-tun geometry and the straining characteristics of the lauter-tun bottom.

As a result of these factors, the practical extract value achievable in a brew house or by an all-grain homebrewer is roughly between 55% and 70%. In German brew houses with modern lauter-tun designs, an extract yield of 75% tends to be norm. This translates into an original gravity (OG) of about 6–8 °Plato (OG 1024–1032) for 1 pound of grain mashed-in with 1 gallon of water.

The original gravity of alt is usually in the vicinity of 11–12 °Plato (OG 1044–1048), with some alt gravities as high as 14 °Plato (OG 1056). If you were to use helles Pils malt only, the *theoretical* grain loading for a standard alt should be roughly between 1.5–2 pounds per gallon, or 45–60 pounds per barrel of wort. But this figure must be adjusted for the practical obstacles to perfect extraction, as discussed previously. Also, the darker the grain, the fewer enzymes it has and the less extract you can expect from it. The actual grain loading required to achieve standard alt gravities, therefore, depends on the combination of the grains you use, on the quality of your grains, and on the extract efficiency that is feasible with your system.

One Düsseldorf alt brewery with an extract efficiency of 75%, for instance, uses about 1.5 pounds of grain per gallon of finished beer, which amounts to about 45 pounds of grain per barrel of beer or 7.5 pounds per 5-gallon batch for an alt wort of 11.8 °Plato (OG 1047). One alt of 13.5 °Plato (OG 1054) was made in two different 30-barrel systems in the United States, with a net yield of about 25 barrels of finished beer. The first system required a grain loading of 68 pounds per barrel of finished beer, the second about 76 pounds. Converted to a 5-gallon batch, this alt might require grain loadings of between 11.3 pounds and 12.5 pounds, depending on the extract efficiency of your system.

A good starting point for a homebrewer is a grain loading of approximately 10 pounds per 5-gallon batch; for the craftbrewer, of approximately 60 pounds per barrel. Then sparge until your kettle gravity (before the start of the boil) is about 10–15% lower than your chosen target wort gravity. This allows for gravity changes from evaporation during the boil. Measure the volume of your yield and the original gravity in your fermenter and, for the next batch, adjust the grain loading upward or downward accordingly.

Mashing

Alt breweries in Germany use either a multistep-infusion process or an infusion in conjunction with a one- or two-step decoction process for mashing, and breweries that use mostly light Pils malt are also more likely to employ decoction in addition to infusion. Total mash times for alt vary from a low of 150 to a high of 170 minutes.

Altbiers, like most German beers, are full bodied. A beer's body comes mostly from degraded, or converted, grain proteins. This conversion is accomplished by a special set of enzymes, called proteolytic enzymes, that reside in the kernel of the grain and become active at temperatures between approximately 113–131 °F (45–55 °C). These enzymes break down large-chain, high-molecular-weight proteins that would flocculate out in the brew kettle or cause chill hazes in the finished beer. After proteolytic conversion, these proteins are rearranged into smaller-chain molecules that tend to survive the kettle boil in greater numbers and do not produce hazes. Converted proteins go by such names as albumins, peptides, and polypeptides.

To accomplish a proteolytic conversion, the German alt brewer must mash-in at a much lower temperature than the British ale brewer. The brewer achieves this by initially infusing the grain with very little hot water (doughing-in) to create a thick mash for what is called the protein rest and then infusing the mash a second time with hot water to bring the grain bed to the next temperature step for the sugar rest. The entire process is called step mashing.

An alt without a protein rest would not be authentic. If you brew your alt with German light malt or an equivalent that is rich in proteins, a single infusion mash may not be sufficient to accomplish the required protein conversion. On the other hand, if you brew your alt with grain that is low in proteins, you may not obtain enough body for an alt even if you employ the correct mashing method.

In a typical British infusion mash, you would fill your mash tun with about 3 pounds of grain per gallon of water. In Düsseldorf, there is a great variation in the grist-to-water ratio among the various altbier breweries.

One brewery, which relies on partial decoction to raise the mash temperature, starts out with a very thin mash, using almost 80% of the kettle volume of water right at the beginning. Another brewery uses about half the kettle volume in water, or about 2 pounds of grain per gallon of mash water, for the initial infusion. A third brewery doughs-in with a grist-to-water ratio of almost 12 pounds of grain per gallon of water (or 375 pounds per barrel), which translates into about one-fifth the kettle volume in water, and then thins out the mash during subsequent infusions.

Altbier decoction mash cooker.

The theoretical drawback to thin starting mashes is the lower concentration of enzymes, but you can start out with a thinner mash if you have top-quality grains with high enzymatic strength. In the North American home- and craftbrew context, where decoction is often not possible and usually not necessary, it is probably best to be on the safe side and start with as thick a mash as your equipment will allow. In a commercial brew house, mash viscosity is often determined by the capabilities of the mash-tun agitator or rake. If the lowest turning speed of the stirring device is higher than 1 or 2 revolutions per minute (rpm) or if it cannot sweep the entire bottom of your mash tun, you should start with a thinner mash.

As a homebrewer, you probably do not have a mash-tun agitator and rely instead on elbow grease and a wooden or plastic paddle for stirring. Doughing-

in, therefore, ought not to be a problem. A thick mash at the protein rest also has the advantage of less thermal mass that needs to be brought up to the next temperature range in a step-infusion regimen. Consequently, you have less of a chance of reaching the volume limit of

Wooden paddle for mixing the mash at home.

your equipment before your grain reaches the required mash-out temperature.

In some Düsseldorf breweries, the temperature regimen for alt mashes starts with a 10- to 20-minute rest at around 99 °F (37 °C), sometimes referred to as an acid rest. This low-temperature rest is often practiced by breweries using a large portion of enzyme-poor dark malts. It enhances starch, enzyme, and protein dissolution (called hydrolysis) and leads to more complete attenuation in the fermenter. It also improves the dissolution of highly viscose hemicellulose (beta-glucan and pentosan), which gives the beer more colloidal stability. Altbiers made with such a rest tend to be more complex but also sharper in flavor. As the name implies, an acid rest acidifies the mash; that is, it lowers its pH value. If you live in a part of North America with highly alkaline water, you might want to consider an acid rest instead of (or in addition to) your brewing liquor treatment. Most alt breweries in Düsseldorf skip the acid rest and select a dough-in or mash-in temperature from 118–128 °F (48–53 °C).

One Düsseldorf brewpub mashes-in for a protein rest of 15 minutes at 118 °F (48 °C), followed by a second 15-minute protein rest at 126 °F (52 °C) and an infusion to bring the grain bed up to the sacchari-fication temperature. Another brewpub goes straight for a 5-minute protein rest at 126 °F (52 °C) and then uses a combination of infusion and decoction to raise the mash temperature. The difference in the mash process explains the difference in the dura-tion of the protein rest. A protein rest of half an hour or even longer (for thinner mashes) is advisable to ensure the completion of pro-teolytic conversion. A good compromise for a North American home- or craftbrewer is to start the alt mash with a 30-minute protein rest at 122 °F (50 °C).

For the temperature change from one rest to the next, commercial breweries often use an infusion of relatively hot water (around 185 °F or 85 °C, or even higher, depending on the thermal absorption charac-teristics of the equipment), or low-pressure steam circulating in jackets through the skin of their mash tuns, or both. A homebrewer is most likely to use a combination of hot-water infusion and direct gas or electric heat. *Always stir the grain bed gently and continuously during temperature increases on the stove* to avoid hot spots that would denature the enzymes and render them useless or could cause scorching of the grain that would both destroy enzymes and add acrid flavors to the beer.

For a textbook alt, successive infusions after the protein rest bring the grain bed up to the following rest temperatures: 144–148 °F (62–64 °C) for the activation of beta-amylase, which are the enzymes that produce simple, fermentable sugars (mostly maltose), 158–162 °F (70–72 °C) for the activation of alpha-amylase, the enzymes that produce complex, unfermentable sugars (mostly dextrins); and 169 °F (76 °C), the mash-out temperature. If you wish to use a single saccharification rest only, a good compromise is a 30-minute rest at 154 °F (68 °C).

Naturally, different alt breweries have their own variations on the sugar-rest theme as well. Breweries that make alt using a multistep-infusion process often employ two saccharification rests, the first at 144 °F (62 °C) for 30 minutes and the second at 162 °F (72 °C) for 20 minutes. Breweries using a traditional decoction process often raise the mash to 153 °F (67 °C) for a single rest of 25 minutes.

Mash-out temperatures in Düsseldorf range from a low of 167 °F (75 °C) after a 20-minute decoction boil of one-third of the mash to a high of 172 °F (78 °C) after a final infusion.

Many North American craftbrewers recirculate their initial runoff from the mash tun back through the grain bed until the wort runs clear. This is rarely done in Germany, where brewers tend to filter or centrifuge their wort before it reaches the fermenter. Because North American home- and craftbrewers probably do not have these commercial methods of wort purification available, you should consider recirculating and whirlpooling your extract if your equipment allows. Recirculation is not a necessity, but it is likely to result in a crisper final product. Chapter 4 contains a few tips on how to rig up a small recirculation system for your homebrew setup.

Boiling

Boiling times for alts vary from 90–120 minutes. Hops are added during the boil in two to four increments and boiled for 45–80 minutes to supply the kettle with a total amount of 80–150 milligrams (mg) of alpha acids per liter of hot wort. At a hops utilization rate of about 30%, this translates into an IBU level of roughly 25–50 IBU.

Boiling times for alt appear somewhat long by North American standards, especially because the additional extraction of alpha acids from the low-alpha hops during the extra boiling time is negligible. Long boiling times, however, create favorable conditions for the browning of the wort and thus for the development of the alt's coppery color. This is the result of the so-called Maillard reaction (see appendix E).

Extract alt brewers have to imitate in the kettle part of the mashing process employed by their all-grain cohorts to obtain the correct color, flavor, and gravity characteristics of their wort. Your unhopped, pale or extra-pale malt extract essentially replaces the pale or Pils foundation grist of the all-grain brewer. The average extract contains about 20% water and 80% sugar. Thus, for a 5-gallon batch, substitute the pale foundation grain with a corresponding amount of extract. For this conversion, assume that 1 pound of extract contains the rough sugar equivalent of 1.3 pounds of milled, two-row, malted grain or, conversely, that 1 pound of two-row grist can be substituted with 0.77 pound of extract. For alt color and flavor, steep the specialty grains in the brewing liquor in your kettle before adding the canned extract. Usually it is not possible to substitute these specialty grains reliably with canned

extract products, as the outcome would be too unpredictable and not yield an authentic alt.

Use the same amounts of specialty grains as indicated for all-grain mashing. By the standards of conventional extract brewing, the amount of grain used with this technique is relatively large. But remember that alt is a copper-colored ale and that you must get most of the alt characteristics (except for texture and body) out of the specialty grains, not out of the can. Steeping your specialty grains produces fewer sugars than does mashing and sparging them; that is, steeping makes only a small contribution to your wort's gravity. For this reason, you have to compensate for the relative loss in gravity by increasing the amount of pale malt extract—usually by about 10–20%—over and above the mathematically determined canned-extract equivalent of the two-row foundation grain only.

To prepare the specialty grains for steeping in the brew liquor, place them first in a strong plastic bag and use a rolling pin or wine bottle to crack them. Do not fine-mill your specialty grains for steeping, as you do not want to leach phenols and unconverted starches into your brewing liquor. After cracking, place the grains in one to three muslin bags—depending on quantity—and immerse them in about 2 gallons of *cold* water. Heat the water *slowly* until you can detect bubbles rising in the kettle. This should take at least half an hour, at which point the brewing liquor should be at about 190° F (88° C). Do not boil your specialty grains! Lift the muslin bag(s) out of the kettle and rinse each with about 1/2 to 1 cup of *cold* water. Do not squeeze the bag(s), because the moisture in the steeped grains is *not* good to the last drop!

After you remove the grains from the kettle, bring the now colored and flavored brewing liquor to a boil. Remove the kettle from the burner to add the extract. This will prevent scorching as the thick extract sinks to the bottom. Stir gently to distribute the extract evenly. Stir *without splashing the wort* to avoid hot-side aeration, which could impart a cardboardlike taste to the beer. Next, bring the mixed wort to a boil. You are now ready for hopping. At this stage, be especially watchful for boil overs, because wort without hops is much foamier.

Hopping

There is a surprisingly large variation in the IBU targets used by German alt makers. Two of the more popular brewpub alts in Düsseldorf have IBU values of 40–42 and 45–48. Other German alts are available with IBU values of 25–27. One alt brewed in the American Northwest has 45 IBU, and another brewed in the Northeast has 25 IBU. Some alts brewed for special occasions may have a hop loading of up to 60 IBU.

It would be neither practical nor even feasible for home- or craftbrewers to quantify the relationship between the alpha-acid ratings of their bittering hops and the composition of their water, on the one hand, and the hop loadings required for specific flavor profiles, on the other. But an understanding of the variables and their interrelationship can focus experimentation and make the interpretation of successive results meaningful (see appendix F). What matters is the proper balance between maltiness and hoppiness, which, in turn, depends mostly on the choice of grains and hops in combination with your brewing water.

The best guideline for the practical brewer is to start with a hops utilization coefficient of 30%, pick the applicable IBU target, and calculate the amount of bittering hops based on kettle volume and alpha-acid ratings, using the formula presented in appendix F. Then experiment with your choice of hops in your system, taste-test the beer, and correct the IBU target for the next batch, if necessary.

Adding Flavor and Aroma Hops

There are no standard rules for calculating the desirable amount of flavor and aroma hops additions. For flavor and aroma, the brewer looks to the hops' volatile oils and their derivatives. The extent to which these oils stay in the wort and become part of the finished beer depends much more on process than on the quantity of hops added near, at, or after the end of the boil. It is a good rule of thumb to add about 1/4 pound of top-quality flavor hop pellets per barrel of alt wort (or about 3 1/2 grams per gallon) at the end of the boil and about 1/2 pound of hop pellets per barrel of wort (or about 7 grams per gallon) in the whirlpool. A few of the smaller alt breweries in Düsseldorf dry hop some of their altbiers in lagering tanks with up to 100–150 grams of leaf hops per hectoliter of wort (about 5 grams per gallon or 5 1/2 ounces per barrel) for extra aroma. In general, though, dry hopping is not very common in German beers.

After a taste test of the finished beer, adjust your hops amounts experimentally for your next brew, depending on the flavor and aroma strength of the hops you use and on your process capabilities. For your aroma yield, consider the temperature of your wort at the whirlpool stage. The lower the temperature, the more of the volatile substances will stay in the wort and the less aroma hops you may need.

Clarifying the Hot Wort

Different breweries use different methods to separate hot trub from hot wort. Whirlpools are common as are hot-wort centrifuges. After the heat exchange to about 54–68 °F (12–20 °C), alt wort is often passed through a diatomaceous-earth wort filter. The wort may also be centrifuged or allowed to cold-sediment before pitching. In North American craftbreweries or at home, wort filtration or centrifuging is probably not even an option, but whirlpooling to remove trub is always a good practice. At home you can whirlpool your wort by hand in the kettle by simply stirring it around repeatedly with a paddle or spoon until the wort spins on its own. But stir gently to avoid aeration of your hot wort!

Aerating the Cooled Wort

To ensure the healthy reproduction of alt yeast, aerate the cold wort until it is completely saturated with oxygen (which occurs when about 10–12 ppm of oxygen are dissolved in the wort). In a craftbrewery, inject filtered air or pure oxygen inline during the entire heat exchange plus about one-half to one hour afterward directly into the fermenter. If you use pure oxygen, set the bottle pressure to no more than 3–4 pounds per square inch (psi).

As a homebrewer, allow the cold wort to drop from the rim of your fermenting vessel. Vigorous shaking of your fermenter (if your back can stand the strain!) provides additional oxygenation for the yeast's reproductive cycle (see appendix D).

Fermenting

The simplest rule for inoculating your green beer with alt yeast is to pitch it at a rate of about 10–20 fluid ounces of "thick" slurry per barrel (0.25–0.5 l/hl), drawn from the bottom of a fermenter. For the homebrewer, the addition of about 0.5–1 fluid ounce of yeast slurry per gallon is a workable approximation. The objective is to have a yeast cell count of 7 to 15 × 10^6 cells/ml in the fresh wort. Some breweries initiate fermentation with up to 25% starter beer to hasten the beginning of high kräusen. Such starters may have a yeast loading of 40 to 60 × 10^6 cells/ml.

Generally, altbier should not be fermented at temperatures exceeding 63 °F (17 °C), though some breweries ferment alt at temperatures as high as 72 °F (22 °C). Alt yeast produces an exceptional amount of foam at temperatures beyond 64 °F (18 °C). At a range of about 64–67 °F (about 18–20 °C), some alt-yeast strains also produce a larger-than-normal amount of sulfuric compounds. The more modern the facility, it seems, the lower are the heat-exchange and fermentation temperatures in use.

Vigorous primary fermentation with alt yeast usually takes three to six days. At 90–92% attenuation, the beer is often transferred to a secondary fermenter, especially if the primary fermenter is open. Temperature settings in closed fermenters vary from one brewery to the next. A good target range for the home- and craftbrewer is 55–65 °F (13–19 °C), but it may be as high as 68 °F (20° C). The temperature is kept constant for the duration of the fermentation. Expect attenuation after the initial burst to progress at an average of about 6–8% per day. To keep alt yeast happy, tank pressure ought not to exceed 8–12 psi (0.6–0.8 bar).

At the end of fermentation, when the brew has reached terminal gravity, it is often cooled by 9–11 °F (5–6 °C) and allowed to rest for 12 hours, after which debris at the bottom of the tank ought to be purged and the yeast harvested. German alt breweries repitch their yeast for about six to twelve months before they breed a fresh colony from pure laboratory-maintained stock.

In some breweries, especially those with higher primary fermentation temperatures, the alt then undergoes a diacetyl rest of two to four days at 57–61 °F (14–16 °C)—after the yeast has been harvested for repitching. During this rest, the remaining yeast count in the brew should still be around 20 to 40 × 10^6 cells/ml. The diacetyl rest entices the yeast to convert any remaining fermentable sugars and, as the name implies, to start re-absorbing diacetyl, a trace element that can give beer a buttery or butterscotch-like taste. During the diacetyl rest, the yeast also reduces aldehydes and changes any unpleasant-tasting fusel alcohols into esters. Because of the increase in beer temperature, the dissipation of sulfides and other disagreeable volatiles is also hastened.

A diacetyl rest is always good practice for any beer, but if you ferment your alt slowly, at the lower end of the temperature range, closer to 55 °F (13 °C), you can skip the diacetyl rest, because the yeast's production of unpleasant trace elements decreases with reduced fermentation speed. For those who like statistics, the diacetyl target value for the finished alt should not exceed 0.1 mg/l. During the diacetyl rest, most breweries purge additional yeast off the tank once or twice. This reduces the chance of autolysis; that is, of the disintegration of dead yeast cells and other organic materials and thus the development of offensive flavors. After the diacetyl rest, the beer is cooled to around 32 °F (0 °C) and transferred for lagering.

Lagering

German alts stay in the cellar much longer than do most British ales, and at lower temperatures. This slows the rate of fermentation and thus reduces the amount of sulfuric and estery compounds released by the yeast into the beer during the stage of vigorous fermentation. During lagering, the yeast then re-absorbs many of these trace elements. Lagering, in this sense, has a similar effect on beer as does a diacetyl rest, except that lagering takes much longer.

Thus you cannot "lager" a beer after it has been filtered. Lagering is always the maturation of beer *on
the yeast*. Note that, in Germany, both ales and lagers
are "lagered."

Conventional lagering cellars for alt maintain an
ambient temperature of 39–41 °F (4–5 °C). In modern breweries, alt is lagered in glycol-chilled tanks at
a temperature in the low 30s–28 °F (approximately
+2– -2 °C). In breweries where the lagering tanks
receive beer directly from open primary fermenters,
the arriving beer may still be at a temperature of
50–64 °F (10–18 °C). In breweries where the tanks
receive beer from modern, closed fermenters, the
beer may already be at the proper lagering temperature. The absolute minimum lagering time for alt is
two weeks, but usually lagering takes much longer.

Filtering

Because alt yeast remains well in suspension, even
fully fermented and lagered alts can still have a large
concentration of yeast with a cell count as high as 15
to 40 × 106 cells/ml. After the alt's first transfer from
the fermenter to the lagering tank, a second transfer
may be necessary after seven to fourteen days of lagering. Many breweries use a centrifuge for a preliminary
clearing of the beer. Final filtration is accomplished
with diatomaceous earth or sheet filters, or both.

Alt-yeast cells have a diameter of about 4–6 microns (μ). A filter with a nominal rated porosity of 3μ—called a polishing filter—is therefore perfectly adequate to clarify an alt. Do not use very sharp filters for a German beer, including an alt, as these remove not only yeast and particulate but also proteins, leaving the beer with a thinner texture then is desirable. So-called sterile filtration—with a sharpness of about 1/2μ—is employed by many brewers of mass beers. Such filtration can even remove color from the beer and lighten it.

Conditioning and Packaging

For packaging, use your standard regimen. If you prime your beer, avoid sugar, which can contribute a slightly sour aftertaste to the brew. Always use light dried malt extract (DME) instead. Before bottling, always chill your alt as much as possible to reduce foaming. If you store your beer in Cornelius kegs, maintain a pressure of about 10–12 psi.

Alt brewpubs in Düsseldorf still use traditional wooden kegs.

90

Altbier breweries in Düsseldorf package their beers in kegs at a carbon dioxide level (CO_2) of approximately 4.2–4.6 g/l. The CO_2 level for bottles is slightly higher, about 5–5.2 g/l. Using standard North American units of measurement for CO_2 levels, these values translate into roughly 2.1–2.2 volumes of CO_2 per volume of beer for kegs and 2.6–2.7 volumes for bottles. If you have a CO_2 tester (most likely to be found in a craftbrewery, not at home), reduce your alt temperature to as close to 28 °F (-2 °C) as possible, and adjust your carbonation to the above values at a tank pressure of about 12 psi.

Some drinkers like their beers very chilled, whereas others prefer their beers almost at room temperature. An alt is best served at a temperature between these two extremes, at about 45 °F (7 °C), to bring out its malty taste and noble hops finish. Alt brewpubs in Düsseldorf store their draft kegs at a cellar temperature of 41 °F (5 °C).

The traditional, swing-top, wire-bale bottle is now hard to find, even in Germany, but several small alt breweries in Düsseldorf still use it for their off-premise sales.

CHAPTER 6

Recipe
Guidelines

This chapter contains brewing guidelines for all-grain (5 gallons and 1 barrel) and extract brews (5 gallons) for the following altbiers: Altstadt Alt (the classic version), Fortuna Alt (a variation on the Düsseldorf theme, with a touch of malted wheat), Rhenish Alt (a slightly nutty and sweet alt), Hanoverian Alt (a darker alt from Lower Saxony), Sticke Alt (a strong Düsseldorf specialty), Enderlein's Alt (a formulation contributed by our technical editor and Düsseldorf brewmaster Herbert Enderlein), Nouvelle Alt (a relatively light version of the alt, created for this book), Westphalian Alt (an alt version with plenty of malted wheat), and Alt Mead (a fun interpretation of the old Germanic mead ale, created for this book). Alt breweries in Germany use a great variety of ingredients and

93

processes to produce their beer. You can choose your own process from the detailed descriptions in chapters 3 and 5 or follow an amalgamated version of the brewing steps as outlined in this chapter. These consolidated process guidelines have been tested, and they have produced authentic results in countless 5-gallon all-grain and extract batches, and in 1-barrel homebrewed all-grain batches. Some of them have also been brewed in commercial batches ranging in size from 7–60 barrels.

Start with a pale malt as your foundation grain (between approximately 50% and 70%). A two-row malt is suitable. If you have a choice, use a grain with a Lovibond rating not exceeding 2° and a protein level of about 12%. If you are an extract brewer, start with a pale or extra pale—preferably lager—extract as your foundation malt. For best results, use an extract imported from Germany. This will satisfy the alt's requirements for body and texture. Always purchase unhopped malt. Extract is nothing but concentrated brewer's wort. As there appear to be no premixed extracts on the market that are specifically formulated for alt, you can substitute only those portions of the grain bill with an appropriate amount of canned extract for which a suitable equivalent is available. As a rule of thumb, consider that 1 pound of canned extract yields the rough sugar equivalent of 1.3 pounds of milled, two-row, malted grain. The grains that cannot be substituted by extract need to be added somehow to the wort to impart their all-important flavor and color characteristics. Thus you will have to steep some specialty grains in your brewing liquor before adding your extract to the brew kettle for the boil.

Extracts often come in cans of 1.5 or 3 kilograms. Three kilograms (6.6 pounds) of extract, therefore, is the equivalent of about 8.5 pounds of two-row malt. Either use the precise quantities of extract needed for 5 gallons of beer (see the recipe guidelines in this chapter) or, if your kettle and fermenter volumes are sufficient, increase the listed amounts of hops and specialty

Brewing up an alt storm at the H&M homebrewery in Osterville, on Cape Cod in Massachusetts.

grains proportionally and brew as much beer as can be made with the full amount contained in your cans. You may also wish to adjust the amount of specialty grains up or down depending on the—usually undisclosed—color value of your extract. If you get your extract from a kit, *do not use the yeast supplied with the kit!* If you have leftover malt extract, transfer it from the can into a plastic container, pour a thin layer of vodka over it, seal it, and store it in the refrigerator. The alcohol in the vodka will prevent mold from growing on the extract surface.

To give the alt its copper color, you can use up to 50% Munich and Vienna malts. You can even add up to about 10–15% crystal malt with a 60 °L rating, provided the crystal does not impart roasted flavor notes. A minuscule amount (perhaps 1–2%) of roasted or black malt is also acceptable in the darker alt versions. The addition of 5–15% wheat malt is optional.

Different altbier breweries in Germany use slightly different temperature steps in the mash tun, but all rely on both a protein rest and one or two saccharification rests. For best results with all-grain formulations at home or in your craftbrewery, dough-in at about 122 °F (50 °C) for a protein rest of about 30 minutes, and then increase the mash temperature, using a combination of hot-water infusion and direct heat, to 148 °F ±2 °F (64 °C ±1 °C) for a beta saccharification rest of about 15 minutes. Next, raise the temperature to 156 °F ±2 °F (69 °C ±1 °C) for an alpha saccharification rest of about 15 minutes, and finally to 170 °F ±2 °F (77 °C ±1 °C) for the mash-out.

All quantities used in the recipe guidelines in this chapter are based on *net kettle volumes,* that is, on the amount of wort that remains in the kettle at the end of the boil. For all-grain batches, the grist amounts are calculated for a low extract efficiency of about 55%. Most home- and craftbrew systems perform better than that, and a few perform worse. If your system's efficiency is known and is different from 55%, adjust your alt grain bill accordingly before you mash in. If it is unknown, measure your net kettle volume instead. If you end up with more than 1 barrel of 5 gallons of wort, respectively, at the correct target gravity, decrease your grain loading proportionally for the next batch. If you end up with less wort, increase it.

Sparge until you reach the alt's target original gravity minus 10–20%, depending on the length and vigor of your boil (to account for evaporation losses). Standard kettle-boiling times for an all-grain alt are 90–120 minutes. For a 90-minute boil, for instance, your kettle gravity should be about OG 1043–1044 for an alt with an OG of 1048. For a 120-minute boil, it should be about OG 1041–1042. The longer the boil, the more likely you will activate the production of melanoidins (see appendix E), which darkens your wort. If you use extract, follow the same rules for your kettle gravity, but shorten the boil to 60 minutes for proper bittering-hops utilization. If the gravity turns out to be too high at the end of the boil, thin your wort with preboiled water.

All-grain brewers who prepare their brewing liquor should note that, in most setups, the total amount of water required for mashing and sparging is roughly 35–55% greater than the net kettle volume. The excess water is lost mostly as discarded run-off after the sparge, as moisture left in the spent grain, and as evaporation during the boil.

You can use Hallertau (Mittelfrüh is best, North American–grown Hallertau worst), Perle, Spalt, or Mt. Hood for bittering, flavor, and aroma. You can use the same hops for all hops additions or select different hops for the different additions. German alt brewers are particularly partial to Hallertau Mittelfrüh, Perle, and Spalt. A good North American–grown substitute is Mt. Hood or domestic Perle. In addition, you can use Tettnanger (of either German or North American origin) as aroma hops. Some alts give a more lingering finishing aroma with Saaz. In the formulations listed in this chapter, the amount of bittering hops is already partially calculated for you (in ounces) using the formula given in appendix F, with an assumed hops utilization of 0.3 and net kettle volumes of 1 barrel and 5 gallons, respectively. To obtain the required amount of bittering hops, divide the number listed in the respective column by the alpha-acid rating listed on the hops package. For flavor hops, use about half the amount as for bittering hops, at shutoff. For aroma hops, use about the same amount as for bittering hops, as the wort starts to cool down in the whirlpool.

Ferment the wort at 60 °F±5 °F (16 °C±3 °C) until it is about 90% attenuated. Use WYEAST 1007, W.G. Kent A06, or an equivalent yeast only. Do not use British or American ale yeasts or German lager yeasts, as these do not produce an authentic alt flavor profile!

At the end of primary fermentation, reduce your fermenter temperature gradually by about 2 °F (1 °C) per day until your alt reaches a lager temperature of 32–40 °F (0–4 °C). Let the alt mature for two weeks to two months on the yeast. Alt gets better with age. During the first two weeks of lagering, you should rack the beer once or twice off the sediment or purge debris out of the bottom of the fermenter.

If you have the equipment, filter (at about 3 microns) before packaging. Package your alt at a temperature as low as possible (down to 28 °F or -2 °C) and at a pressure not exceeding 12 psi. Store it at about 41 °F (5 °C) and serve it at about 45 °F (7 °C).

Altstadt Alt

Here is a typical alt that you might find in the old town of Düsseldorf, the altstadt, where almost every building contains an altbier pub.

Altstadt Alt has a medium-copper color and a full body, a light hoppy nose, a malty middle flavor, and a medium-dry finish.

Malt (%)	All-grain bbl.	All-grain 5 gal.	Extract 5 gal.
Two-row malt (60%)	36 lbs.	6 lbs.	—
Munich (15%)	9 lbs.	1.5 lbs.	1.5 lbs.
Vienna (15%)	9 lbs.	1.5 lbs.	1.5 lbs.
Crystal 60 °L (10%)	6 lbs.	1 lb.	1 lb.
Pils malt extract (unhopped)	—	—	5 lbs.
Total grain	60 lbs.	10 lbs.	—

Hops	All-grain 1 bbl.	All-grain 5 gal.	Extract 5 gal.
Bittering	0.554 ÷ %AA oz.	0.089 ÷ %AA oz.	0.089 ÷ %AA oz.
Flavor	2.9 oz. (80 g)	0.5 oz. (13 g)	0.5 oz. (13 g)
Aroma	5.75 oz. (160 g)	1 oz. (27 g)	1 oz. (27 g)

Alt Specifications

Bittering hops:	Hallertau Mittelfrüh, Mt. Hood, Perle, or Spalt
Flavor hops:	Hallertau Mittelfrüh, Mt. Hood, Perle, or Spalt
Aroma hops:	Spalt or Tettnanger (or Saaz for a more aromatic finish)
Yeast:	WYEAST 1007 (or equivalent)
IBU:	40*
SRM:	18*
OG:	12 °P (1048)*
FG:	2.5 °P (1010)*
ABV:	4.8%*

*Nominal values. Actual values may differ, depending on your ingredients and process variables. For an explanation of these variables, see chapter 5 and appendices E and F.

Fortuna Alt

Fortuna is the name of Düsseldorf's soccer club. *Fortuna* is a Latin word meaning luck, fate, or fortune. Düsseldorf's beer, like its soccer team, has seen its fortunes wane and wax, but both have held their own over time.

Fortuna Alt is made with a small addition of malted wheat. It has a brilliant coppery hue and a lingering, aromatic, dry hop finish.

Malt (%)	All-grain1 bbl.	All-grain 5 gal.	Extract 5 gal.
Two-row (72.5%)	42 lbs.	7 lbs.	—
Crystal 60 °L (15%)	7.5 lbs.	1.5 lbs.	1.5 lbs.
Caramel (7.5%)	4.5 lbs.	0.5 lb.	0.75 lb.
Wheat malt (5%)	3 lbs.	0.5 lb.	0.5 lb.
Pils malt extract (unhopped)	—	—	6 lbs.
Total grain	57 lbs.	9.5 lbs.	

Hops	All-grain 1 bbl.	All-grain 5 gal.	Extract 5 gal.
Bittering	0.346 ÷ %AA oz.	0.056 ÷ %AA oz.	0.056 ÷ %AA oz.
Flavor	1.7 oz. (48 g)	0.25 oz. (8 g)	0.25 oz. (8 g)
Aroma	3.6 oz. (102 g)	0.6 oz. (17 g)	0.6 oz. (27 g)

Alt Specifications

Bittering hops:	Hallertau Mittelfrüh, Mt. Hood, Perle, or Spalt
Flavor hops:	Hallertau Mittelfrüh, Mt. Hood, Perle, or Spalt
Aroma hops:	Spalt or Tettnanger
Yeast:	WYEAST 1007 (or equivalent)
IBU:	25*
SRM:	20*
OG:	12 °P (1048)*
FG:	3 °P (1012)*
ABV:	4.6%*

*Nominal values. Actual values may differ, depending on your ingredients and process variables. For an explanation of these variables, see chapter 5 and appendices E and F.

Rhenish Alt

This alt is slightly sweet and nutty. It is reminiscent of alts made in the Lower Rhineland between Düsseldorf and the Dutch border.

Rhenish Alt has no noticeable bouquet, but a strong, yet mellow, up-front hoppiness and a satisfying middle maltiness.

Malt (%)	All-grain 1 bbl.	All-grain 5 gal.	Extract 5 gal.
Two-row malt (39.5%)	27.5 lbs.	4.5 lbs.	—
Munich (35%)	24.5 lbs.	4 lbs.	4 lbs.
Vienna (20%)	14 lbs.	2.25 lbs.	2.25 lbs.
Crystal 60 °L (5%)	3.5 lbs.	0.5 lb.	0.5 lb.
Black (0.5%)	0.5 lb.	1.5 oz.	1.5 oz.
Pils malt extract (unhopped)	—	—	4 lbs.
Total grain	70 lbs.	11.25 lbs.	—

Hops	All-grain 1 bbl.	All-grain 5 gal.	Extract 5 gal.
Bittering	0.374 ÷ %AA oz.	0.06 ÷ %AA oz.	0.06 ÷ %AA oz.
Flavor	2 oz. (54 g)	0.3 oz. (9 g)	0.3 oz. (9 g)
Aroma (Tettnanger)	2 oz. (54 g)	0.3 oz. (9 g)	0.3 oz. (9 g)
Aroma (Perle or Spalt)	4 oz. (108 g)	0.6 oz. (18 g)	0.6 oz. (18 g)

Alt Specifications

Bittering hops:	Hallertau Mittelfrüh, Mt. Hood, Perle, or Spalt
Flavor hops:	Hallertau Mittelfrüh, Mt. Hood, Perle, or Spalt
Aroma hops:	Tettnanger and Perle or Spalt
Yeast:	WYEAST 1007 (or equivalent)
IBU:	27*
SRM:	19*
OG:	12.5 °P (1050)*
FG:	3 °P (1012)*
ABV:	4.8%*

*Nominal values. Actual values may differ, depending on your ingredients and process variables. For an explanation of these variables, see chapter 5 and appendices E and F.

Hanoverian Alt

The altbiers of Hanover are relatively dark and strong, though light-bodied. They have very little nose and are low in hop flavor. They are often drunk fortified with a clear, vodka-like schnapps.

Malt (%)	All-grain 1 bbl.	All-grain 5 gal.	Extract 5 gal.
Two-row (57.5%)	32 lbs.	5.5 lbs.	—
Crystal 60 °L (30%)	16 lbs.	3 lbs.	3 lbs.
Munich (7.5%)	4 lbs.	0.75 lb.	0.75 lb.
Vienna (5%)	3 lbs.	0.5 lb.	0.5 lb.
Pils malt extract (unhopped)	—	—	5.25 lbs.
Total grain	55 lbs.	9.75 lbs.	—

Hops	All-grain 1 bbl.	All-grain 5 gal.	Extract 5 gal.
Bittering	0.317 ÷ %AA oz.	0.051÷ %AA oz.	0.051 ÷ %AA oz.
Flavor	1.7 oz. (48 g)	0.25 oz. (8 g)	0.25 oz. (8 g)
Aroma	3.2 oz. (90 g)	0.5 oz. (15 g)	0.5 oz. (15 g)

Alt Specifications

Bittering hops:	Hallertau Mittelfrüh, Mt. Hood, Perle, or Spalt
Flavor hops:	Hallertau Mittelfrüh, Mt. Hood, Perle, or Spalt
Aroma hops:	Spalt or Tettnanger
Yeast:	WYEAST 1007 (or equivalent)
IBU:	23*
SRM:	33*
OG:	12–12.5 °P (1048 to 1050)*
FG:	2.5 °P (1010)*
ABV:	4.1–5.1%*

*Nominal values. Actual values may differ, depending on your ingredients and process variables. For an explanation of these variables, see chapter 5 and appendices E and F.

Sticke Alt

Düsseldorf alt brewpubs make seasonal specialty alts in small batches as surprises for their customers. These alts give the alt brewmasters a chance to experiment and create their own variations on the standard theme. Known in the local dialect as *sticke* (secret) or *latzenbier* (slab beer), specialty alts are usually a bit stronger, darker, and hoppier (up to 60 IBU) than regular alts. They are served as long as the supply lasts—rarely more than a few days.

This Sticke Alt is well balanced. It has a light hoppy nose, a good middle maltiness, and a surprisingly dry finish in spite of its high gravity.

Malt (%)	All-grain 1 bbl.	All-grain 5 gal.	Extract 5 gal.
Two-row (46%)	30 lbs.	5.25 lbs.	—
Munich (23%)	15 lbs.	2.5 lbs.	2.5 lbs.
Caramel (7.5%)	5 lbs.	0.75 lb.	0.75 lb.
Crystal 60 °L (21%)	13.5 lbs.	2.5 lbs.	2.5 lbs.
Black 500 °L (2.25%)	1.5 lbs.	0.25 lb.	0.25 lb.
Pils malt extract	—	—	6.6 lbs. (2 kg)
Total grain	65 lbs.	11.25 lbs.	—

Hops	All-grain 1 bbl.	All-grain 5 gal.	Extract 5 gal.
Bittering	0.692 ÷ %AA oz.	0.112 ÷ %AA oz.	0.112 ÷ %AA oz.
Flavor	3.6 oz. (102 g)	0.6 oz. (17 g)	0.6 oz. (17 g)
Aroma	7.3 oz. (204 g)	1.2 oz. (34 g)	1.2 oz. (34 g)

Alt Specifications

Bittering hops:	Hallertau Mittelfrüh, Mt. Hood, Perle, or Spalt
Flavor hops:	Hallertau Mittelfrüh, Mt. Hood, Perle, or Spalt

Aroma hops:	Spalt or Tettnanger
Yeast:	WYEAST 1007 (or equivalent)
IBU:	50*
SRM:	57*
OG:	13.5 °P (1056)*
FG:	3.5 °P (1014)*
ABV:	5.3%*

*Nominal values. Actual values may differ, depending on your ingredients and process variables. For an explanation of these variables, see chapter 5 and appendices E and F.

Enderlein's Alt

This alt formulation is supplied by Mr. Herbert Enderlein, the technical editor of this book and brewmaster at Brauerei Ferdinand Schumacher, the oldest altbier brewery in Düsseldorf (Schumacher opened its doors in 1838).

For all-grain batches, this alt requires only one type of grain, a two-row Pils malt kilned to a pale Munich color rating of 6.5 °L. If you cannot obtain Munich malt with such a low color rating, blend a small portion of two-row pale malt into your grain bill. To calculate the relative amounts, use the formula in appendix E.

For extract batches, the given quantities are based on a 3-kilogram can (6.6 pounds) of Pils malt extract with a color rating of approximately 2 °L and some 5.75 pounds of milled 6.5 °L Munich malt for steeping. Depending on the actual color rating of your ingredients, you may have to adjust these quantities to obtain an 11–12 °L altbier. With a 10 °L Munich malt, for instance, you have to steep only 3.75 pounds of milled grain to achieve the same color value.

The malt in this beer is balanced by only two hop additions of Hallertau Mittelfrüh—one for bitterness, one for aroma.

Malt (%)	All-grain 1 bbl.	All-grain 5 gal.	Extract 5 gal.
Munich 6.5 °L (100%)	56 .5 lbs.	9 .25 lbs.	5.75 lbs.
Pils malt extract	—	—	6.6 lbs.
Total grain	56 .5 lbs.	9 .25 lbs.	—

Hops	All-grain 1 bbl.	All-grain 5 gal.	Extract 5 gal.
Bittering	0.554 ÷ %AA oz.	0.089 ÷ %AA oz.	0.089 ÷ %AA oz.
Flavor	—	—	—
Aroma	5.75 oz. (160 g)	1 oz. (27 g)	1 oz. (27 g)

Alt Specifications

Bittering hops:	Hallertau Mittelfrüh
Flavor hops:	None
Aroma hops:	Hallertau Mittelfrüh
Yeast:	WYEAST 1007 (or equivalent)
IBU:	40*
SRM:	11–12*
OG:	11.7 °P (1047)*
FG:	2.5 °P (1010)*
ABV:	4.8%*

*Nominal values. Actual values may differ, depending on your ingredients and process variables. For an explanation of these variables, see chapter 5 and appendices E and F.

Nouvelle Alt

Düsseldorf has always had a smidgen of French influence. Nicknamed Little Paris, it has become one of Germany's most prominent fashion centers. One of the streets leading to the altstadt is called Kaiser-straße, or Emperor Street, so named after the French emperor Napoleon, who triumphantly entered the city by this road in 1811. Ironically, Napoleon was seen then as the liberator of Europe, who promised to free the Old Continent from its repressive, absolute monarchs. A few years later, the tide turned against him and he was seen instead as the scourge of Europe. Napoleon's favorite watering hole in Düsseldorf was an old tavern, Zum Schiffchen, which has been in business since 1628 and still serves altbier today.

Nouvelle Alt is a light and very blonde haute couture alt, created for this book for the fashion- and calorie-conscious set. We call it Nouvelle Alt in spite of the contradiction in terms. It has a very mild hop nose; subdued up-front bitterness; a medium body with pleasant maltiness; and a gentle, dry hop finish.

Malt (%)	All-grain 1 bbl.	All-grain 5 gal.	Extract 5 gal.
Two-row (80%)	40 lbs.	6.5 lbs.	—
Munich (15%)	6 lbs.	1 lb.	1 lb.
Vienna (5%)	4 lbs.	0.5 lb.	0.5 lb.
Pils malt extract	—	—	5.5 lbs.
Total grain	50 lbs.	8 lbs.	

Altbier

Hops	All-grain 1 bbl.	All-grain 5 gal.	Extract 5 gal.
Bittering	0.222 ÷ %AA oz.	0.036 ÷ %AA oz.	0.036 ÷ %AA oz.
Flavor	1.1 oz. (30 g)	0.2 oz. (5 g)	0.2 oz. (5 g)
Aroma	2.4 oz. (66 g)	0.4 oz. (11 g)	0.4 oz. (11 g)

Alt Specifications

Bittering hops:	Hallertau Mittelfrüh, Mt. Hood, Perle, or Spalt
Flavor hops:	Tettnanger
Aroma hops:	Saaz
Yeast:	WYEAST 1007 (or equivalent)
IBU:	16*
SRM:	11*
OG:	10 °P (1040)*
FG:	3.75 °P (1011)*
ABV:	3.7%*

*Nominal values. Actual values may differ, depending on your ingredients and process variables. For an explanation of these variables, see chapter 5 and appendices E and F.

Westphalian Alt

This alt is unusual for its large portion of malted wheat, which gives the beer a slightly sour, refreshing taste. Try this beer *mit schuß*, the German practice of mixing about a tablespoon of fruit syrup, such as raspberry, strawberry, or boysenberry, with the beer in the glass.

Westphalian Alt has a slightly pale-golden color, a medium body, a noticeable up-front maltiness, and a middle hop flavor. It has a dry finish reminiscent of a spritzy wheat beer and a lingering, balanced, hoppy-malty aftertaste.

Malt (%)	All-grain 1 bbl.	All-grain 5 gal.	Extract 5 gal.
Two-row (50%)	30 lbs.	5 lbs.	—
Munich (10%)	5 lbs.	1 lb.	1 lb.
Malted wheat (40%)	25 lbs.	4 lbs.	4 lbs.
Pils malt extract	—	—	4.5 lbs.
Total grain	55 lbs.	10 lbs.	—

Hops	All-grain 1 bbl.	All-grain 5 gal.	Extract 5 gal.
Bittering	0.278 ÷ %AA oz.	0.045 ÷ %AA oz.	0.045 ÷ %AA oz.
Flavor	1.5 oz. (42 g)	0.25 oz. (7 g)	0.25 oz. (7 g)
Aroma	3 oz. (84 g)	0.5 oz. (14 g)	0.5 oz. (14 g)

Alt Specifications

Bittering hops:	Hallertau Mittelfrüh, Mt. Hood, Perle, or Spalt
Flavor hops:	Tettnanger
Aroma hops:	Saaz
Yeast:	WYEAST 1007 (or equivalent)
IBU:	20*
SRM:	10*
OG:	11 °P (1044)*
FG:	3 °P (1012)*
ABV:	4%*

*Nominal values. Actual values may differ, depending on your ingredients and process variables. For an explanation of these variables, see chapter 5 and appendices E and F.

Alt Mead

The Germanic tribes of 2,000 years ago often flavored their ales—forerunners of the alt—with aromatic herbs and honey. This interpretation of what such a brew might have tasted like was created specifically for this book and does not exist commercially. It relies for part of its flavor on English hops—otherwise not suitable for alt making—to imitate the more floral

Altbier

quality of wild herbs. Choose your own hops types and quantities with alpha-acid ratings that suit your palate. In the adventurous spirit of true home- and craftbrewing, this alt-based brew is intended for fun and experimentation only and lays no claim to authenticity of any sort.

Malt (%)	All-grain 1 bbl.	All-grain 5 gal.	Extract 5 gal.
Two-row malt (57%)	36 lbs.	6 lbs.	—
Munich (11.5%)	7.5 lbs.	0.25 lb.	1.25 lbs.
Malted wheat (14%)	9 lbs.	1.5 lbs.	1.5 lbs.
Caramel (5%)	3 lbs.	0.5 lb.	0.5 lb.
Crystal 60° L (11.5%)	7.5 lbs.	1.25 lbs.	1.25 lbs.
Black (0.75%)	0.5 lb.	1.5 oz.	1.5 oz.
Honey	3 lbs.	0.5 lb.	0.5 lb.
Pils malt extract (unhopped)	—	—	5 lbs.
Total grain	63.5 lbs.	12 lbs.	—

Hops Amounts	All-grain 1 bbl.	All-grain 5 gal.	Extract 5 gal.
Bittering (E. Kent Golding)	4.25 oz. (120 g) @ 5%AA	0.75 oz. (20g) @ 5%AA	0.75 oz. (20 g) @ 5%AA
Bittering (Tettnanger)	4.25 oz. (120 g) @ 4.2%AA	0.75 oz. (20g) @ 4.2%AA	0.75 oz. (20 g) @ 4.2%AA
Flavor	4.25 oz. (120 g)	0.5 oz. (20 g)	0.5 oz. (20 g)
Aroma	6.5 oz. (180 g)	1 oz. (30 g)	1 oz. (30 g)

Alt Specifications
Bittering hops:	East Kent Golding and Tettnanger
Flavor hops:	Tettnanger
Aroma hops:	Fuggle
Yeast:	WYEAST 1007 (or equivalent)
IBU:	30*
SRM:	33*
OG:	14–14.5 °P (1056–1058)*
FG:	3.5–4 °P (1014–1016)*
ABV:	5.2–5.6%*

*Nominal values. Actual values may differ, depending on your ingredients and process variables. For an explanation of these variables, see chapter 5 and appendices E and F.

Commercial Alt Examples

Alaskan Amber

Brewed in Juneau, Alaska, this amber is really an alt. It is relatively low in hop flavor and has a dry finish.

Diebels Alt

Brewed in Issum, just outside Düsseldorf, this is one of the fuller-bodied alts with a deep-copper color and a faintly roasty note in the finish. Diebels ranks among the market leaders of the style.

Dornbusch Alt

Brewed in Ipswich, Massachusetts, this alt balances malty sweetness with smooth bitterness. A North American representation of a typical Düsseldorf pub-style alt, it is available in 12-ounce bottles as well as in 1-liter, wire-bale-top bottles.

Düssel Alt

Named after the Düssel, the little river that flows through the old town of Düsseldorf and then empties into the Rhine, this alt is a Düsseldorf original. Unlike most alts, Düssel has a faint note of estery fruitiness that is more reminiscent of a British than a German ale.

Frankenheim Alt

A Düsseldorf original, Frankenheim represents the lighter-colored but hoppier interpretation of the style.

Füchschen Alt

Brewed at the altbier brewpub Im Füchschen at 28 Ratingerstraße in the old town of Düsseldorf, this alt has a brilliant copper color and a lingering, aromatic, dry hop finish. This brewpub also sells its beer in half-liter bottles with a wire-bale top.

Grolsch Amber

Brewed not in the Rhineland but in neighboring Holland, this amber Dutch ale is a rather dark, malty, hoppy version of an altbier and one of the few European alts widely available in North America.

Hannen Alt

One of the best-selling alts in Germany, Hannen is brewed in Mönchengladbach and Willich, in the Lower Rhineland between Düsseldorf and the Dutch border. Hannen is smooth and mellow with a slightly malty finish.

Pinkus Alt

Brewed in Münster in Westphalia, this alt is unusual for its large portion of wheat (about 40%) in the grain bill. As a result, the beer has a golden rather than copper color and a slightly sour finish.

Rhenania Alt

Brewed in the Lower Rhineland town of Krefeld, near the Dutch border, this alt is very full bodied and ranks among the heavier-tasting alts.

Schlösser Alt

A Düsseldorf original, Schlösser has a deep copper color, very low hoppiness, and a malty, dry finish.

Schlüssel Alt and Gatzweiler Alt

At the brewpub Zum Schlüssel at Bolker-straße 43 in the old town of Düsseldorf, this alt is available on tap. In bottles, it is available in stores under the name Gatzweiler. This alt is slightly malty-sweet with a sharp finish.

Schmalz's Alt

Brewed in New Ulm, Minnesota, this alt is fairly dark-malty with an unusual, slightly roasty, chocolate finish.

Schumacher Alt

Brewed in the oldest altbier brewpub in Düsseldorf (and thus probably in the world), Schumacher has a great balance between maltiness and aromatic hoppiness. The pub, located at 123 Oststraße, just outside the old town, also sells its beer over the counter in 1-liter, wire-baletop bottles.

St. Stan's Amber

Brewed in Modesto, California, this amber is an alt by a different name. It is very malty with a slightly aromatic hop finish.

Uerige Alt

Brewed in one of the classic old-town brewpubs, at 1 Bergerstraße in Düsseldorf, Uerige is very hoppy and aromatic and has a long-lasting, malty finish. Uerige Alt is also available in half-liter bottles with the traditional wire-bale top.

Widmer Alt

Brewed in Portland, Oregon, this alt is reminiscent of its Düsseldorf model, balancing maltiness with assertive hop bitterness.

Malting German Grain

In the old days, brewing malts were made in direct-heat kilns fueled by wood, coal, or coke. These malts were invariably dark and smoky from fuel residues. But in the early nineteenth century, top-quality malts began to be dried by indirect heat. The burners in these modern kilns heat clean air that is blown into the malting stations. This allows for precise temperature control and the production of extremely pale malts completely free of off-flavors.

The German beer-purity law, the Reinheitsgebot, not only regulates the ingredients in beer, but also dictates what maltsters may or may not do. Chemical cleaning agents and germination enhancers that are legal in many countries are strictly forbidden in Germany. Thus German maltsters must achieve naturally what others often accomplish with the aid of modern food science. The following is a conventional malting schedule for German light or Pils (helles) malt as it appears in the standard texts that German master-brewer students must internalize at a university.

Light Pils Malting

Pils malt is usually moistened for 24–48 hours at 54–68 °F (12–20 °C). Some maltsters extend the moistening period to as much as seven days, whereby the temperature is gently raised to about 64 °F (18 °C) and then allowed to drop to about 56 °F (13.5 °C). This slow germination process produces a malt of thorough and even (but not excessive) modification. It also yields a high enzyme content.

After steeping, the malt is lightly dried in three stages. During the first cycle, which takes about 10–15 hours, the temperature is increased gradually from 113 to 131 °F (45 to 55 °C).

During the second cycle, the grain-bed temperature is raised in increments of 9 °F (5 °C) per hour to about 176 °F (80 °C).

During the third drying cycle, the grain is kept at 176–185 °F (80–85 °C) for an additional 4–5 hours, depending on the desired color.

Once the grain has reached the proper color in the kiln, it is allowed to cool for about 2–5 hours. The entire malting process for light malt takes a minimum of about 40–75 hours, but it can take as much as eight days.

Vienna Malting

Vienna malts—made from the same barley as light Pils malts—undergo the same three-step kilning process as do light malts. Vienna malt takes on its characteristic color only during the final drying cycle, when it is subjected to a temperature of 185–203 °F (85–95 °C) for 3–4 hours.

Munich Malting

Munich (dark) malt, too, comes from the same raw material and is treated very similarly to light Pils malt, but obtains its color by undergoing a longer, three-step drying sequence.

The first kilning cycle lasts for about 2–6 hours at 99–116 °F (37–48 °C), during which the grain bed is exposed to moist, recirculating air with an initial relative humidity of 45%. The humidity is never allowed to drop below 30%. This process ensures that the resulting grain is sufficiently modified; that is, its proteins have already begun to hydrolyze and to degrade.

The second cycle takes 6 hours at above 140 °F (60 °C) with step-increases in temperature to 176° F (80 °C) and a quick jump to 212 °F (100 °C) at the end.

During the third and final drying cycle, Munich malt is roasted at a temperature of 216–221 °F (102–105 °C) for up to 4–5 hours, whereby the roasting time and temperature vary depending on the desired color value of the grain (between 8 °L and 12 °L).

Mash pH and
Water Hardness

The acronym pH—which stands for potential hydrogen—denotes the degree of acidity or alkalinity of a solution on a scale from 1 to 14, whereby a pH of 7 indicates a neutral solution (that is the pH of distilled water). A pH of 1 is the most acidic, and 14 is the most alkaline (or caustic) solution. The pH scale is not linear but logarithmic, which means that each increase or decrease by one pH point makes the solution ten times more acidic or alkaline. For instance, a mash of pH 3 is ten times more acidic than a mash of pH 4 and 100 times more acidic than a mash of pH 5. For those who are truly curious about the nefarious mechanisms at work in the connection between water hardness/softness and mash pH, the (inevitably) tortuous explanation follows.

The alkalinity reading of water is usually given in parts per million (ppm) or milligrams per liter (mg/l), which are two identical ways of measuring the same substance. It is expressed either as mg/l of bicarbonates (HCO_3) or as mg/l of calcium carbonate ($CaCO_3$); whereby 40% of the latter compound is calcium and 60% is CO_3. Confusingly, bicarbonates are also referred to as "temporary hardness," which precipitates during the boil. In plain English, calcium carbonate is known as precipitated chalk. The thing to remember is that temporary hardness, regardless of how it is measured, raises the mash pH (makes the mash more alkaline).

Now things get complicated, because the experts do not use terms and concepts consistently and thus make it difficult for us ordinary folk to read even a simple chart that compares water specifications from different famous brewing centers around the world. Depending on the compound (bicarbonate or calcium carbonate) in which alkalinity is expressed, the numerical value is different for the same water. The value of water alkalinity expressed in bicarbonates is approximately 40% lower than the alkalinity value for the same water expressed in calcium carbonate.

The other compounds—also expressed in ppm or mg/l—that play a role in determining the mash pH are calcium and magnesium (written either as Ca and Mg or, with their positive ion designations, as Ca^{++} and Mg^{++}). This is called "permanent hardness," which does not precipitate during the boil. The presence of calcium and magnesium ions lowers the mash pH, making the mash more acidic. The combination of bicarbonate, calcium, and magnesium ions in the water determines what is called the water's "residual alkalinity" or "total alkalinity," which, in turn, affects the pH of a given mash. In Europe, water hardness is usually expressed in °dH (which stands for *deutsche Härte,* or German hardness). The conversion factor is 1 °dH = 17.9 ppm calcium carbonate.

Sugar Fungus:
Plant or Animal?

Next time you are at a party where people play "20 questions," stymie the crowd with this one: *protist*. They will never get past the bit about vegetable, animal, or mineral.

As brewers we have all worked with protists and experienced both their desirable and their devastating effects. In the scheme of biological classification, protists are single-cell organisms that scientists have not been able to anchor firmly into either the plant or the animal kingdom. They rank somewhere in between. Both yeasts and bacteria are protists. Both can ferment wort, but only yeast can produce clean-tasting beer, whereas bacteria spoil it.

Yeasts, including the brewer's yeasts *Saccharomyces cerevisiae* and *Saccharomyces uvarum*, are protists of a higher order, which scientists call eukaryotes. Eukaryotes are distinguished by the presence of cell nuclei and the ability to reproduce by cell division. Bacteria, by comparison, belong in the category of prokaryotes. Prokaryotes are protists of a lower order that lack true cell nuclei. For the brewer, *Saccharomyces* has two important life cycles: a reproductive phase and a metabolic phase. Under aerobic conditions—that is, in aerated wort—yeast reproduces itself vigorously through cell division. Under anaerobic conditions—that is, when all the oxygen in the wort is used up—yeast "eats," or metabolizes (ferments), sugars. After fermentation, yeast goes dormant, until it is reintroduced to fresh wort with new sugar to start the cycle again.

The Latin word for yeast, *Saccharomyces*, means "sugar fungus." But not all yeast can metabolize all sugars! Also known as saccharides, sugars are by far the most important brewing hydrocarbons derived from the grain.

Sugars are classified by their molecular complexity. Sugars with one to three molecules are generally fermentable by brewer's yeast, whereas sugars with four or more molecules generally are not. Fermentable saccharides are the source of alcohol and carbon dioxide in beer, and unfermentable saccharides stay in the finished beer as residual sugars and contribute to the beer's body, mouthfeel, and head. "Dry" or "light" beers are those without residual sugars.

Monosaccharides are single-molecule sugars such as glucose and fructose. Disaccharides are two-molecule sugars such as maltose, sucrose (common table sugar, composed of one glucose and one fructose molecule), and melibiose. Trisaccharides are three-molecule sugars such as maltotriose and raffinose (a sugar composed of two melibiose molecules and one fructose molecule). Oligosaccharides are sugars of four or more molecules (complex sugars). Polysaccharides are complex sugars that are capable of being reduced to fermentable monosaccharides, and dextrins are polysaccharide fractions that cannot be reduced to fermentable saccharides by either ale or lager yeasts.

All ale yeasts, including alt yeast, can ferment sugars with one to three molecules, except for the melibiose portion of raffinose, whereas all lager yeasts can ferment melibiose molecules as well. This accounts in part for the difference in taste between ales and lagers. So-called wild yeasts, which tend to create undesirable off-flavors in beer, are super-attenuators that can ferment even dextrins. The most important sugars in the average wort are fructose (1–2%), sucrose (4–8%), glucose (8–10%), maltotriose (12–18%), and maltose (46–50%).

Calculating Your Grain Bill for Beer Color

In North American texts about brewing, the color of beer is usually given in °SRM, which stands for degrees Standard Research Method, a standard adopted by the American Society of Brewing Chemists. This standard is based on spectrophotometric principles, which measure the ability of a substance to absorb light. The Europeans, unfortunately, use a different standard for measuring beer color. It, too, is based on spectrophotometry, but it is calculated based on a reference light of a different wavelength. European color values are expressed in °EBC (which stands for degrees European Brewing Convention).

North American malting companies usually give the color of their grains in °L, which stands for degrees Lovibond, so named after J. W. Lovibond, who created the scale in 1883. In theory, 1 °L equals 1 °SRM for a grain-to-water ratio of 1 pound per gallon. To convert °EBC into °L (and thus °SRM) and vice versa, malt suppliers use the following formulas:

$$1 \text{ °L (or 1 °SRM)} = 1 \text{ °EBC} \times 0.375 + 0.46$$
$$1 \text{ °EBC} = 1 \text{ °L (or 1 °SRM)} \times 2.67 - 1.23$$

The numerical identity between grain color measured in °L and beer color measured in °SRM, however, is only an approximation, because several practical considerations interfere with the theoretical validity of the mathematical model. As a general rule, as your target beer color deepens, so must its combined grain color.

To figure out the combined color rating of a particular grain bed, we must calculate the contribution each grain makes to the color of the wort, because each grain in the grist colors the finished beer in proportion to both its Lovibond rating and its relative share of the overall grain bill. If we adjust this combined Lovibond value of the grain bed by the volume of wort extracted from the grain, we have a useable nominal color value for the finished beer. In other words, the darker the specialty grains or the larger the amount of dark specialty grains in the grain bill, the darker will be the wort. Likewise, a small volume of wort extracted from a given grain bill is darker and heavier than a larger volume of wort extracted from the same grain bill. To calculate the combined Lovibond rating of a grain bed made up of different grains with different color ratings, plug the Lovibond values and the amounts of the different grains as well as the net kettle volume at the end of the boil into the following formula:

$$(°L_1 \times lb_1 + °L_2 \times lb_2 + °L_3 \times lb_3 + ... + °L_n \times lb_n) \div V_{Knet}$$

whereby

1, 2, 3, ..., n are the different grains
$°L_1, °L_2, °L_3, ..., °L_n$ are the Lovibond ratings of these grains
$lb_1, lb_2, lb_3, ..., lb_n$ are the amounts (in pounds) of each grain
V_{Knet} is the volume of wort (in gallons) at the end of the boil

Multiply the Lovibond rating in °L for each grain by its weight in pounds (lb.) and add these products into one sum. Once you divide this sum by the volume of wort (in gallons), you have an approximate nominal SRM color rating of the finished beer obtainable from this grain bill under ideal conditions.

Example

Grain (°L)	Amount (lbs.)	Amount (%)	(°L × lbs.)
Two-row (1.68 ° L)	32.00 lbs.	56.14%	53.76
Munich (5 °L)	18.50 lbs.	32.46%	92.50
Caramel (15.46 °L)	4.00 lbs.	7.02%	62.72
Crystal (56.7 °L)	2.00 lb.	3.51%	113.40
Black (530 °L)	0.50 lb.	0.88%	286.20
Total	57.00 lbs.	100.00%	608.58

Kettle net volume 31 gallons = 1 barrel
Nominal SRM beer color value: 608.58 ÷ 31 = 19.63 °SRM

In this example, the resulting beer has a nominal color value of about 19.5 °SRM. For altbier, you should compose your grain bill so that the nominal color value (that is, its combined Lovibond rating per gallon of wort) is roughly 13–20 °SRM. Depending on the shade of copper you desire in your alt, select a higher (darker) or lower (lighter) number for your grain bill.

Several process factors conspire to make the nominal beer color value based on the composition of the grain bed only a rough guide of the actual color value of the finished beer. Such process influences are more noticeable in blonder or paler brews than they are in darker brews. They include such variables as the length of the boil, the heat source of your kettle (steam or direct fire, which can caramelize and thus darken the brew), and the material from which your kettle is made (copper darkens the wort more than does stainless steel, for instance). If you are an extract brewer who relies on a concentrated wort boil, consider that higher-viscosity worts (that is, higher-gravity worts) have a greater darkening effect on your beer because of the inevitable caramelization in your brew kettle.

Perhaps the most significant process effect on beer color is the browning that comes from so-called melanoidins. These are the product of an oxidation-reduction process, called the Maillard reaction, that requires heat and moisture. The reaction starts when the grain is being malted, at a kilning temperature of

176–185 °F (80–85 °C). It is interrupted once the grain is fully dried in the kiln, but it resumes in the kettle and continues until the beer starts to ferment. The Maillard reaction consists of a complex sequence of chemical processes. During the first part (called Amadori rearrangement), sugars and amino acids in the grain combine to form new complexes. During the second part (called Strecker reduction), these complexes are degraded into aldehydes. The aldehydes, in turn, are then transformed into melanoidins, which function as browning agents that deepen the color of the wort and thus of the beer.

Melanoidin production during the kettle boil of the wort is the more prolific, the longer the boil lasts. In bock beers, for instance, which require a boil of several hours, it is the Maillard reaction that is chiefly responsible for the deep amber color of the beer. Because the Maillard reaction continues in the wort, once it is re-initiated during the boil, beer also becomes darker the longer the hot wort is kept in the whirlpool. For the same reason, malt extracts, too, keep getting darker the longer they are stored in a can. This is why it is best to buy your malt extract only from stores with good inventory turnover and to use your cans soon after you buy them.

Calculating Your Bittering Hops Addition

Bittering in wort or beer is measured in International Bittering Units (IBU) or their conversion into other measurement systems, such as Homebrew Bittering Units (HBU). One IBU is defined as 1 milligram of dissolved iso-alpha-acids (isohumulones) in 1 liter of wort or beer. One HBU is defined as 1 ounce (28 grams) of a 1%AA hop. Because HBU do not relate to the volume of wort or beer, no mathematical correlation exists between HBU and IBU. The human taste threshold for bitterness is 4 IBU. The solubility limit for iso-alpha-acids in cold beer is approximately 100 IBU.

Once you know the target IBU value of your beer, you can calculate kettle hops additions (in ounces or pounds) based on your kettle volume (V) in gallons, the hop's alpha-acid rating (%AA) supplied by the grower, and the hop utilization coefficient (U), which you have to guess. Assume that your hops utilization is 30% (or 0.3). Brew your first batch, taste it, and adjust your utilization figure upward or downward accordingly. A convenient formula for the North American home- and craftbrewer is:

Bittering hops (oz.) = (V × IBU) / (U × %AA × 7,462), whereby 7,462 is a calculation constant that converts mg/l into oz./gal.

To obtain the amount of bittering hops in pounds for larger batches, simply divide the result by 16.

Example 1
V = 1 bbl. (= 31 gal.)
IBU = 23
U = 30% (= 0.3); this is our best guess!
%AA = 3.9% (= 0.039)

Calculation of bittering hops by weight:

[(1 bbl. kettle volume × 31 gallons × 23 IBU) divided by (0.3 utilization × 0.039 AA × 7,462)] divided by 16 = (713 / 87.3054) / 16 = 8.168 / 16 = 0.51

For this brew, you would use approximately 1/2 pound of bittering hops.

Example 2
V = 5 gal.
IBU = 40
U = 0.3
%AA = 3.4%

Calculation of bittering hops by weight:

(5 gal. kettle volume × 40 IBU) divided by (0.3 utilization × 0.034 AA × 7,462) = 200 / 76.1124 = 2.63

For this brew, you would use approximately 2 1/2 ounces of bittering hops.

Some authors offer more complicated formulas that include such factors as gravity correction values and the contributions of second, third, and subsequent hop additions to the aggregate amount of bittering compounds in the finished beer. It is true that hops utilization decreases as wort viscosity increases; that is, with higher wort gravities. It is also true that hop additions late in the boil contribute small amounts of alpha acids to the wort. But as is apparent from the discussion about that all-important factor of hops utilization (on page 133), any such mathematical complications—though analytically defensible— merely fine-tune a value that is largely based on guesswork. On a practical level, our formula is about as accurate and as meaningful as possible within the home- and craftbrewing context for altbiers with a gravity in the range of OG 1044–1054.

Unlike kettle volumes, which are easily measured, and alpha-acid ratings, which are listed on the hops package, true hops utilization is a frightfully devilish quantity to deal with. In theory, hops utilization expresses the percentage of bittering compounds that reach the final beer compared to the overall amount of bittering compounds added to the wort during the brewing process. It is the laboratory-measured amount of iso-alpha-acids in the beer divided by the amount of alpha acids added to the wort. In practice, unfortunately, many factors conspire to make the true utilization coefficient of hops in your system more a matter of guesswork than of exact analysis.

Hops utilization can vary greatly. For a 60-minute boil, for instance, it may vary between 15% and 20% for leaf hops and between 10% and 30% for pellets. The length and vigor of the boil can also affect the amount of alpha acids extracted from the hops, as can the kettle geometry and the thermodynamics it produces. If you are an extract brewer who relies on a concentrated wort boil, calculate the amount of bittering hops based on the *final* kettle volume, not on the volume of concentrated wort, and keep in mind that hops utilization deteriorates with increasing wort viscosity. Thus, you must compensate for your utilization losses by adding perhaps as much as an extra 10% of bittering hops to your calculated amount.

As a rough guideline, about half the bittering compounds that are attainable with your process in your system are extracted into the wort during the first 30 minutes of the boil, with ever smaller additional amounts being extracted for every additional 10-minute interval. Because of this diminishing return of bittering compounds per boil length, boiling times beyond 60 minutes are often employed for other reasons, such as a kettle-gravity increase through evaporation or a deliberate browning of the wort through the production of melanoidins (see appendix E), as is the case in Düsseldorf, where many alt brewers boil their wort from 90–120 minutes. A longer boiling time often improves beer flavor by promoting a more thorough coagulation of unwanted wort material as well as the evaporation of wort off-flavors up the brew stack.

Because alpha acids can oxidize under less than perfect storage conditions, hops utilization based on the original %AA as stated on the package by the hops supplier is likely to deteriorate as hops get older. After one year, for instance, especially leaf hops may have lost as much as one-third of their original alpha-acid content, even if properly stored in a sealed container in the refrigerator. The loss may be up to one-half after about two years.

Hops utilization may also decrease as you add larger quantities of low-alpha bittering hops as opposed to smaller quantities of high-alpha bittering hops to your wort. Alts brewed in Germany are usually made with German-grown hops. These varieties tend to have fewer alpha acids per weight (usually between 2.5% and 3.5%) than do the same or similar varieties grown in North America (which tend to have between 4% and 6%). If you use German hops, such as Halltertau Mittelfrüh, an alpha-acid content greater than 2.8% is desirable. Depending on the vagaries of the weather, German alpha-acid ratings can be as low as 1.5% in certain years (when German growers destroy rather than sell their harvest) and North American ratings as high as 9% for comparable varieties. To put these figures in perspective, remember that some of the "super-bitterers" used by North American brewers, such as Chinook, Galena, or Nugget, may have as much as 16%AA.

Because bittering-hop additions are calculated based on your measured kettle volume, on a fixed length of the boil (60 minutes, for instance), on an assumed hops utilization (we use 30% for starters), and on an alpha-acid rating stated by the supplier, you often need to add comparatively more German-grown than North American–grown hops by weight to your wort to achieve the same IBU target. Adding larger amounts of lower-alpha hops compared to smaller quantities of higher-alpha hops, however, also introduces a relatively greater concentration of polyphenols, such as tannins, into the wort. These, in turn, can reduce hop utilization rates through a complicated chain of events, as described in the following paragraph.

Polyphenols tend to form complexes with proteins, of which there is no shortage in German Pils malts. At the beginning of the boil, these proteins are dissolved in the wort. Because of their molecular weight, the complexes formed by polyphenols and proteins precipitate to the bottom as the kettle boil progresses. In this process, the precipitating proteins, unfortunately, attach themselves to alpha acids, usually before the acids have a chance to isomerize and become wort-soluble. In other words, alpha acids in the embrace of sinking proteins and their polyphenol mates are lost for good. Although they were added to the wort, we will never taste them in the beer; that is, they represent a loss in utilization.

Because the true hops utilization of a given brew normally cannot be predicted with certainty by the practical home- or craftbrewer, it is often advisable to leave the utilization coefficient constant (at 30%) when calculating the required amounts of bittering hops. Then, if need be, adjust the IBU target experimentally in successive brews.

Bittering hops not only impart bitterness to the beer, but also leave a host of other trace elements in the wort that survive boiling, fermenting, and filtering. Just as maltiness balances hoppiness, so do these other elements affect the beer's flavor profile.

Water hardness, too, influences *perceived* bitterness. In the Rhineland, water hardness is about 200–250 ppm. In New England, by comparison, a water hardness of 60 ppm is not uncommon, which lowers hop bitterness perception substantially. If your brew water is naturally soft, or if you treat your brew water to eliminate hardness, you should adjust your target IBU value upward, and vice versa.

Unit Conversion Chart

Index	lb. to kg	oz. to g	fl. oz. to ml	gal. to l US	gal. to l UK
0.25	0.11	7	7	0.95	1.14
0.50	0.23	14	15	1.89	2.27
0.75	0.34	21	22	2.84	3.41
1.00	0.45	28	30	3.79	4.55
1.25	0.57	35	37	4.73	5.68
1.50	0.68	43	44	5.68	6.82
1.75	0.79	50	52	6.62	7.96
2.00	0.91	57	59	7.57	9.09
2.25	1.02	64	67	8.52	10.23
2.50	1.13	71	74	9.46	11.36
2.75	1.25	78	81	10.41	12.50
3.00	1.36	85	89	11.36	13.64
3.25	1.47	92	96	12.30	14.77
3.50	1.59	99	103	13.25	15.91
3.75	1.70	106	111	14.19	17.05
4.00	1.81	113	118	15.14	18.18
4.25	1.93	120	126	16.09	19.32
4.50	2.04	128	133	17.03	20.46
4.75	2.15	135	140	17.98	21.59
5.00	2.27	142	148	18.93	22.73
5.25	2.38	149	155	19.87	23.87
5.50	2.49	156	163	20.82	25.00
5.75	2.61	163	170	21.77	26.14
6.00	2.72	170	177	22.71	27.28
6.25	2.84	177	185	23.66	28.41
6.50	2.95	184	192	24.60	29.55
6.75	3.06	191	200	25.55	30.69
7.00	3.18	198	207	26.50	31.82
7.25	3.29	206	214	27.44	32.96
7.50	3.40	213	222	28.39	34.09
7.75	3.52	220	229	29.34	35.23
8.00	3.63	227	237	30.28	36.37
8.25	3.74	234	244	31.23	37.50
8.50	3.86	241	251	32.18	38.64
8.75	3.97	248	259	33.12	39.78
9.00	4.08	255	266	34.07	40.91
9.25	4.20	262	274	35.01	42.05
9.50	4.31	269	281	36.96	43.19
9.75	4.42	276	288	37.91	44.32
10.00	4.54	283	296	37.85	45.46
10.25	4.65	291	303	38.80	46.60
10.50	4.76	298	310	39.75	47.73
10.75	4.88	305	318	40.69	48.87
11.00	4.99	312	325	41.64	50.01
11.25	5.10	319	333	42.58	51.14
11.50	5.22	326	340	43.53	52.28
11.75	5.33	333	347	44.48	53.41
12.00	5.44	340	355	45.42	54.55

By Philip W. Fleming and Joachim Schüring.   Reprinted with permission from *Zymurgy*®.

Appendix G

qt. to l		pt. to l		tsp.	tbsp.	cup
US	UK	US	UK	to ml	to ml	to ml
0.24	0.28	0.12	0.14	1.2	3.7	59
0.47	0.57	0.24	0.28	2.5	7.4	118
0.71	0.85	0.35	0.43	3.7	11.1	177
0.95	1.14	0.47	0.57	4.9	14.8	237
1.18	1.42	0.59	0.71	6.2	18.5	296
1.42	1.70	0.71	0.85	7.4	22.2	355
1.66	1.99	0.83	0.99	8.6	25.9	414
1.89	2.27	0.95	1.14	9.9	29.6	473
2.13	2.56	1.06	1.28	11.1	33.3	532
2.37	2.84	1.18	1.42	12.3	37.0	591
2.60	3.13	1.30	1.56	13.6	40.2	651
2.84	3.41	1.42	1.70	14.8	44.4	710
3.08	3.69	1.54	1.85	16.0	48.1	769
3.31	3.98	1.66	1.99	17.3	51.8	828
3.55	4.26	1.77	2.13	18.5	55.4	887
3.79	4.55	1.89	2.27	19.7	59.1	946
4.02	4.83	2.01	2.42	20.9	62.8	1,005
4.26	5.11	2.13	2.56	22.2	66.5	1,065
4.50	5.40	2.25	2.70	23.4	70.2	1,124
4.73	5.68	2.37	2.84	24.6	73.9	1,183
4.97	5.97	2.48	2.98	25.9	77.6	1,242
5.20	6.25	2.60	3.13	27.1	81.3	1,301
5.44	6.53	2.72	3.27	28.3	85.0	1,360
5.68	6.82	2.84	3.41	29.6	88.7	1,419
5.91	7.10	2.96	3.55	30.8	92.4	1,479
6.15	7.39	3.08	3.69	32.0	96.1	1,538
6.39	7.67	3.19	3.84	33.3	99.8	1,597
6.62	7.96	3.31	3.98	34.5	103.5	1,656
6.86	8.24	3.43	4.12	35.7	107.2	1,715
7.10	8.52	3.55	4.26	37.0	110.9	1,774
7.33	8.81	3.67	4.40	38.2	114.6	1,834
7.57	9.09	3.79	4.55	39.4	118.3	1,893
7.81	9.38	3.90	4.69	40.7	122.0	1,952
8.04	9.66	4.02	4.83	41.9	125.7	2,011
8.28	9.94	4.14	4.97	43.1	129.4	2,070
8.52	10.23	4.26	5.11	44.4	133.1	2,129
8.75	10.51	4.38	5.26	45.6	136.8	2,188
9.99	10.80	4.50	5.40	46.8	140.5	2,248
9.23	11.08	4.61	5.54	48.1	144.2	2,307
9.46	11.36	4.73	5.68	49.3	147.9	2,366
9.70	11.65	4.85	5.82	50.5	151.6	2,425
9.94	11.93	4.97	5.97	51.8	155.3	2,484
10.17	12.22	5.09	6.11	53.0	159.0	2,543
10.41	12.50	5.20	6.25	54.2	162.6	2,602
10.65	12.79	5.32	6.39	55.4	166.3	2,662
10.88	13.07	5.44	6.53	56.7	170.0	2,721
11.12	13.35	5.56	6.68	57.9	173.7	2,780
11.36	13.64	5.68	6.82	59.1	177.4	2,839

Glossary

abv. Abbreviation for "alcohol by volume." See *alcohol*.

abw. Abbreviation for "alcohol by weight." See *alcohol*.

adjuncts. Any unmalted cereal, such as rice or corn, added to beer as a starch substitute for malted barley or malted wheat.

aeration. The process by which sterile air (or pure oxygen) is pumped through fresh wort that is inoculated with yeast to stimulate the yeast's reproductive cycle. See *pitching* and *yeast*.

aerobic. Life processes that require oxygen. Yeast has two phases of life, an aerobic and an anaerobic phase. In the presence of oxygen, yeast cells multiply. In the absence of oxygen, they ferment (i.e., metabolize) sugars into alcohol, carbon dioxide, and other trace elements.

alcohol. A product of fermentation. The type of alcohol produced by the yeast varies with yeast strain, yeast health, fermentation temperature, and fermentation method. The desired alcohol in beer is ethanol. So-called higher alcohols have a higher boiling point than ethanol and can leave a "fusel" flavor in the beer. Alcohol is measured by weight (abw) or by volume (abv). Abv is the volume of alcohol as a percentage of the volume of beer, in which it is in solution. Abw is the weight of alcohol as a percentage of the weight of the beer, in which it is in solution. The abw figure is roughly 20% lower than the abv figure for the same beer, because a given amount of alcohol weighs less than the equivalent amount of water.

ale. Any beer that is fermented with a strain of *Saccharomyces cerevisiae*. These are so-called top-fermenting yeasts, most of which work best at temperatures from approximately 60–75 °F (16–24 °C). Alt yeasts can work down to a temperature of 55 °F (13 °C).

alpha acids. A type of hop resin that undergoes a change in its molecular structure (see *isomerization*) when it is boiled in the wort. The resulting compounds, iso-alpha-acids, give the beer its up-front bitterness.

amylase. A group of enzymes that reside naturally in the grain and convert unfermentable grain starches into sugars (see *diastatic enzymes*). The most important of these enzymes are alpha-amylase and beta-amylase. Alpha-amylase specialize in producing complex sugars called dextrins, which generally are not fermentable by the yeast. Beta-amylase specialize in producing simple sugars, which generally are fermentable by the yeast.

anaerobic. Life processes that occur in the absence of oxygen.

attenuation. A quantitative measurement of the reduction of the specific gravity of wort as a result of fermentation. Prior to fermentation, a particular wort might have 12% extract. As fermentation progresses, more and more sugars are converted into alcohol and carbon dioxide. As a result, the wort gets "lighter," or more attenuated, until fermentation stops and the wort has a residual extract of, perhaps, 3–4%. At this point, the beer is fully attenuated.

barrel. In brewing, a U.S. barrel holds 31 U.S. gallons (1.17 hectoliters), whereas a British barrel holds 36 imperial gallons (1.63 hectoliters).

beer. Any alcoholic, undistilled drink made mostly from grain. Its main subcategories are ale and lager.

Biersteuergesetz. The German beer-tax law, which regulates not only the tax rate paid by brewers, but also the ingredients and processes permitted in malting grain and brewing beer.

carbonates. Alkaline salts whose negative ions are derived from carbonic acid.

carbonation. The amount of carbon dioxide gas (CO_2) dissolved in finished beer. The more carbon dioxide is in the beer, the more effervescent the beer is. Excessive carbonation produces a "burpy," gassy beer. Too little carbonation produces a flat, pallid beer. Carbon dioxide is a natural by-product of the yeast's fermentation. In a normal wort, the yeast produces more carbon dioxide than is needed for the finished beer. At the beginning of fermentation, therefore, carbon dioxide is allowed to escape the fermenter. At the end of fermentation, brewers often "cap" (that is, close) the fermenter to develop pressure in the beer tank and keep the remaining carbon dioxide dissolved in the beer. Before bottling or kegging beer, brewers usually correct its carbon dioxide content to the proper level by either bleeding off any excess or injecting additional amounts under pressure.

carbon dioxide (CO_2). A gas composed of carbon and oxygen. Next to alcohol, carbon dioxide is the most important product of yeast fermentation. See *carbonation*.

cerevisia. Latin word meaning "beer." Still used in the scientific name for ale yeast, *Saccharomyces cerevisiae.*

chill haze. Cloudiness in beer caused by suspended proteins and tannins (see *proteins* and *tannins*). The breakup of large proteins into small proteins by proteolytic enzymes is designed to reduce or eliminate chill hazes from protein. Careful timing of the length of sparging can prevent the excessive leaching of tannins from the grain and thus reduce chill hazes from this source. A good rolling boil in the brew kettle also helps to reduce chill hazes by coagulating proteins and colloiding tannins with proteins so that both may precipitate out of the wort. Gums and cellulose are grain carbohydrates that can increase wort viscosity and form hazes in the beer, unless these are properly degraded by enzymatic action in the mash tun. Regardless of the source of hazes, sharp filtration after fermentation can eliminate such hazes before the beer reaches the consumer.

decoction. The process by which part of the mash is removed, heated in a cooker, and then returned to the main mash to raise its temperature. Decoction aids in enzymatic action and the conversion of starches into sugars in poorly modified grains. See *modification*.

dextrins. Complex sugars that cannot be fermented by brewer's yeast.

diastatic enzymes. Starch-converting substances in the grain that work as catalysts. They cause a chemical reaction in starch molecules without being themselves part of the resulting new compounds—sugars. The most important function of mashing is the activation of diastatic enzymes.

dunkel. German word meaning "dark." Usually refers to a dark Bavarian lager.

enzymes. Protein-based organic substances that cause chemical changes in the compounds upon which they act. See *diastatic enzymes* and *proteolytic enzymes*.

esters. Aromatic compounds created through the interaction of organic acids with alcohol. In beer, they are created by enzymes in the yeast during fermentation and are often responsible for fruitiness or a bananalike flavor in the finished beer. Different yeast strains have different propensities for ester production. Ester production generally also increases with increased fermentation temperatures. Esters can be detected in low concentrations and are, to some extent, acceptable in certain British ales but generally not in German alts or lagers.

ethanol. The standard form of alcohol produced by brewer's yeast under normal conditions.

extract. The sugar-containing runoff from the mash tun. Extract also contains proteins, minerals, vitamins, flavor substances, and other trace elements from the grain. Its strength is measured as a percentage of dissolved substances (that is, everything other than water) in the runoff.

fermentation. The process by which yeast converts sugars into alcohol and carbon dioxide.

flocculation. The process by which yeast cells aggregate and sediment to the bottom of the tank after fermentation.

grist. Milled or cracked grain, before it is placed in the mash tun.

gruit. Old German word meaning "wild herbs," usually yarrow, bog myrtle, or juniper. Used to flavor beer until the early Middle Ages, before hops came into wide use. The term *gruit* eventually became synonymous with the tax every medieval German household had to pay to the authorities in exchange for the right to collect herbs and brew beer.

head. The foamy, white layer on top of the brew, after the beer is poured into a glass. The head is made up mostly of proteins, dextrins (see *sugars*), and carbon dioxide. A good head is considered essential in a quality alt.

hell (helles). German word meaning "light" (in color only). Usually a blonde lager.

hofbräuhaus. A feudal court brew house, usually associated with a pub. In the old days, a great source of revenue for monopoly-minded overlords.

hops. A clinging vine whose female flowers are used to give beer bitterness, flavor, and aroma.

hybrid yeast. A misnomer frequently applied to alt yeast strains, whose metabolic characteristics seem to place them halfway between British ale and German lager yeasts. In biology, true hybrids, however, are offsprings of two plants or animals of different species. Referring to alt yeasts as hybrids implies that they are crosses between ale yeasts (*Saccharomyces cerevisiae*) and lager yeasts (*Saccharomyces uvarum*), which they are not. Alt yeasts are true representatives of *Saccharomyces cerevisiae.*

hydrolysis. The process by which substances (such as starches) are made water-soluble. This occurs in mashing, when starches are hydrolyzed to make them accessible to enzymes, which convert starches to sugars.

infusion. The process by which grain is "infused" with hot water during mashing. During step infusion, the grain bed is infused twice or several times with water of different temperatures. The object is usually to activate proteolytic enzymes first, beta-amylase (a diastatic enzyme) second, and alpha-amylase (also a diastatic enzyme) last.

isomerization. A process by which an organic compound changes its molecular structure but not its weight and composition. Under the influence of a vigorous boil, the alpha acids extracted from the hops change to iso-alpha-acids, which account for most of the bitterness in beer. See *alpha acids* and *hops*.

keutebier. A medieval hopped wheat ale made mostly in northern Germany.

kilning. The process of drying the grain after malting. The longer the kilning time and the higher the kilning temperature, the darker is the resulting brewing grain (and beer made from it) and the smaller is the number of enzymes that can be re-activated in the mash tun. Highly kilned malt must always be mixed in the mash tun with enzyme-rich pale malt to have a sufficient concentration of enzymes for diastatic and proteolytic conversion. See *diastatic enzymes* and *proteolytic enzymes*.

lager. From the German word *lagern*, "to store." Any beer fermented with strains of *Saccharomyces uvarum* (see *yeast*), which work best at temperatures around 50 °F (10 °C). After fermentation, lagers are aged, or cold-conditioned, for several weeks to several months. Lagering near the freezing point helps to precipitate yeast and proteins and generally mellows the beer's taste. In Germany, altbiers—though ales—are also lagered.

lautering. From the German word *läutern*, "to clear or clarify." The process of draining the sugar-rich extract from the grain bed in the mash tun.

malt. Grain that has been malted. See *kilning* and *malting*.

malting. The process of steeping grain and allowing it to partially germinate. Germination is interrupted by kiln drying the grain. During malting, a portion of the grain's enzymes are activated. During the mashing of the grain in the brew house, the activation of the grain's enzymes continues.

malz. German word meaning "malt."

mashing. The process of steeping grain in hot water in the mash tun to hydrolyze (see *hydrolysis*) carbon-based and nitrogen-based substances, degrade haze-forming proteins (see *proteolytic enzymes*), and convert starches into sugars (see *diastatic enzymes* and *sugars*).

modification. A process that occurs during malting. It is a measure of the degree to which grain proteins have become soluble in water as a result of enzymatic action.

pasteurization. Heating the packaged beer to 140–175 °F (60–80 °C) for at least 20 minutes to make it microbiologically stable and extend its shelf life.

pH. Abbreviation for "potential hydrogen." It expresses the degree of acidity or alkalinity of a solution on a logarithmic, that is, nonlinear, scale of 1 to 14, whereby 1 is extremely acidic, 7 is neutral, and 14 is extremely caustic. Diastatic enzymes generally work best at a mash pH of roughly 5–5.5.

phenols. Aromatic building blocks of polyphenols and tannins, which can contribute to stale or medicinal flavors in beer and to chill hazes.

pitching. The process of introducing yeast, usually drawn in a thick slurry from a previously fermented batch, into fresh wort.

protein rest. The time required during mashing for proteolytic enzymes to become active and convert large-molecular proteins into small-molecular proteins.

proteins. Organic compounds whose basic building blocks are amino acids (formed from nitrogen) and carbon skeletons. The degradation of proteins during kilning and mashing frees amino acids. These are important as yeast nutrients. They affect yeast health and metabolism and thus the flavor and quality of the finished beer. See *yeast.*

proteolytic enzymes. Protein-converting substances in the grain that work as catalysts. They cause a chemical change in protein molecules, called proteolysis, without being themselves part of the resulting new compounds. During proteolysis in the mash tun, these specialized enzymes convert large proteins in the grain into small proteins. Small proteins are less likely to coagulate and precipitate in the brew kettle or get trapped in the beer filter. To the extent that they reach the finished beer, they contribute to its body and head.

racking. The process of transferring wort or beer from one tank to another or into kegs.

Reinheitsgebot. The German beer-purity decree issued first in Bavaria in 1516. It stipulated that only barley, hops, and water could be used in beermaking. The function of yeast in fermentation was not known at that time. Since then, the Reinheitsgebot has been amended. It now insists that all barley used be "malted." It also allows for malted wheat in wheat ales and includes yeast as a beermaking ingredient.

rest. Holding the mash at a specific temperature for a specific time to induce enzymatic reactions.

saccharification. The process by which malt starch is converted into sugars, mostly maltose.

sparging. The process of sprinkling hot water over the grain bed during lautering until all the sugars are extracted from the grain.

sugars. Also known as saccharides, sugars are by far the most important brewing hydrocarbons derived from the grain. Sugars with one to three molecules are generally fermentable by brewer's yeast, whereas sugars with four or more molecules generally are not. Monosaccharides are single-molecule sugars such as glucose and fructose. Disaccharides are two-molecule sugars such as maltose and melibiose. Trisaccharides are three-molecule sugars such as maltotriose and raffinose. Oligosaccharides are sugars of four or more molecules (complex sugars). Polysaccharides are complex sugars that are capable of being reduced to fermentable monosaccharides, and dextrins are polysaccharide fractions that cannot be reduced to fermentable saccharides.

sugar rest. The time required during mashing for diastatic enzymes to become active and convert starches into sugars.

tannins. Astringent phenolic substances in the grain and hops. If present in excess, tannins may impart a medicinal flavor to the finished beer.

trub. From the German word *trübe*, which means "murky." The sediment of coagulated proteins, hop resins, polyphenols, vegetable gums, hop fibers, and other debris that accumulates at the bottom of the brew kettle during the boiling of the wort.

water hardness. General hardness—often expressed as mg/l of calcium carbonate ($CaCO_3$)—is a measure of calcium and manganese ions dissolved in the water. Bicarbonate hardness, also known as temporary hardness, is a more specific measure of bicarbonates (HCO_3) dissolved in the water. The combination of bicarbonate, calcium, and magnesium ions in the water also determine what is called the water's residual alkalinity.

wort. The sweet extract that is boiled in the brew kettle and, after the addition of hops, becomes unfermented beer.

yeast. The Latin word for yeast, *saccharomyces*, means "sugar fungus." Brewer's yeasts fall into two categories, *Saccharomyces cerevisiae* (ale yeasts) and *Saccharomyces uvarum* (lager yeasts). Under aerobic conditions, yeast reproduces itself vigorously through cell division. Under anaerobic conditions, yeast "eats," or metabolizes, sugars—a process we call fermentation. After fermentation, yeast goes dormant, until it is reintroduced to fresh wort with new sugar (see *pitching*) to start the cycle again.

References and Further Reading

Altenbach, Tom. "Put Your Grain to Work." *Zymurgy*, Special 1995 (Vol. 18, No. 4).

American Homebrewers Association. *Winners Circle*. Boulder, Colo.: Brewers Publications, 1989.

Beach, David. *Homegrown Hops*. Junction City, Ore.: David R. Beach, 1988.

Bishop, Morris. *Middle Ages*. Boston: Houghton Mifflin, 1987.

Bloch, Marc. *Feudal Society*, volumes 1 & 2. London: Routledge & Kegan, 1991.

"Brauerei Schumacher, 1838–1988." Pamphlet published by Schumacher Brauerei on the occasion of the brewery's 150th anniversary. Düsseldorf, Germany: Schumacher Brauerei, September 1988.

Bridgwater, William, and Elizabeth Sherwood, eds. *The Columbia Encyclopedia*, 2nd ed. New York: Columbia University Press, 1950.

Broderick, Harold, ed. *The Practical Brewer*. Madison, Wis.: Master Brewers Association of the Americas, 1977.

Burch, Byron. "Of Yeast and Beer Styles." *Zymurgy*, Special 1989 (Vol. 12, No. 4).

Busch, Ernst. *Vom Beginn der Französischen Revolution 1789 bis zur Gegenwart*. 12th ed. Frankfurt: Diesterweg, 1965.

Butcher, Alan D. *Ale & Beer: A Curious History*. Toronto: McClelland & Steward, 1989.

Cone, Clayton. "Commercial Production of Dried Yeast." *Zymurgy*, Special 1989 (Vol. 12, No. 4).

Daniels, Ray. *Designing Great Beers*. Boulder, Colo.: Brewers Publications, 1996.

Davidson, Darwin E. "Bitterness Basics." *Zymurgy*, Special 1997 (Vol. 20, No. 4).

Davis, Norman. *Europe: A History*. New York: Oxford University Press, 1996.

Denke, Kurt. "Fleischmann (aka Budweiser) Yeast." *Zymurgy*, Special 1989 (Vol. 12, No. 4).

Deschner, Roger. "The Regal Altbiers of Düsseldorf." *Zymurgy*, Winter 1994 (Vol. 17, No. 5).

Dornbusch, Horst. *Prost!: The Story of German Beer*. Boulder, Colo.: Brewers Publications, 1997.

Eckhardt, Fred. *The Essentials of Beer Style*. Portland, Ore.: Fred Eckhardt Communications, 1989.

―――. "Beer Traditions of Old Germany." *Zymurgy*, Special 1993 (Vol. 16, No. 4).

―――. "German Style Ale." *Zymurgy*, Special 1991 (Vol. 14, No. 4).

―――. "The Hybrid Styles: Some Notes on Their Fermentation and Formulation." *Zymurgy*, Special 1989 (Vol. 12, No. 4).

Eden, Karl. "History of German Brewing." *Zymurgy*, Special 1993 (Vol. 16, No. 4).

Ehrenfels-Mehringen, Erich v. *Gambrinus*. Duisburg, Germany: Carl Lange, 1953.

―――. "Yeast Stock Maintenance and Starter Culture Production." *Zymurgy*, Special 1989 (Vol. 12, No. 4).

Farnsworth, Paul. "Healthy Homebrew Starter Cultures." *Zymurgy*, Special 1989 (Vol. 12, No. 4).

Farrell, Norman. "The Enchanting World of Malt Extract—Make the Most of It." *Zymurgy*, Winter 1994 (Vol. 17, No. 5).

Fix, George. *Principles of Brewing Science.* Boulder, Colo.: Brewers Publications, 1989.

————. "Wild Yeast." *Zymurgy,* Special 1989 (Vol. 12, No. 4).

Fix, George, and Laurie Fix. *Oktoberfest, Vienna, Märzen.* Classic Beer Style Series No. 4. Boulder, Colo.: Brewers Publications, 1991.

Foster, Terry. *Pale Ale.* Classic Beer Style Series No. 1. Boulder, Colo.: Brewers Publications, 1990.

————. *Porter.* Classic Beer Style Series No. 5. Boulder, Colo.: Brewers Publications, 1992.

Frane, Jeff. "Modern Altbier Demands Old Techniques." *Brew Your Own,* October 1996 (Vol. 2, No. 10).

Friedrich, Ernst. *Bier.* Künzelsau, Germany: Sigloch, 1993.

Garetz, Mark. *Using Hops.* Danville, Calif.: Hop Tech, 1994.

Gerlach, Wolfgang, Hermann Gutmann, Michael Hassenkamp, Udo Moll, and Werner Widmann. *Das deutsche Bier.* Hamburg, Germany: HB Verlags- und Vertriebsgesellschaft, 1984.

Gesellschaft für Öffentlichkeitsarbeit der Deutschen Brauwirtschaft e.V., ed. *Vom Halm zum Glas.* Bonn, Germany: no date.

Gold, Elizabeth, ed. *Evaluating Beer.* Boulder, Colo.: Brewers Publications, 1993.

Gruber, Mary Anne. "Inspecting Your Malt." *The New Brewer,* March–April 1994 (Vol. 11, No. 2).

Guinard, Jean-Xavier. "Lambic: A Unique Combination of Yeasts and Bacteria." *Zymurgy,* Special 1989 (Vol. 12, No. 4).

Guinard, Jean-Xavier, Mary Miranda, and Michael Lewis. "Yeast Biology and Beer Fermentation." *Zymurgy,* Special 1989 (Vol. 12, No. 4).

Hall, Michael L. "What's Your IBU?" *Zymurgy,* Special 1997 (Vol. 20, No. 4).

Hellex, Rolf. *Bier im Wort.* Nürnberg, Germany: Carl, 1981.

Heyse, Karl-Ulrich. *Handbuch der Brauereipraxis*, 3rd ed. Nürnberg, Germany: Carl, 1994.

Hillman, Howard. *The Gourmet Guide to Beer*. New York: Washington Square Press, 1983.

Isenhour, John. "A Sterile Transfer Technique for Pure Culturing." *Zymurgy*, Special 1989 (Vol. 12, No. 4).

Jackson, Michael. *The New World Guide to Beer*. Philadelphia: Running Press, 1988.

———. *Michael Jackson's Beer Companion*. Philadelphia: Running Press, 1993.

———. *The Simon and Schuster Pocket Guide to Beer*, 6th ed. New York: Simon and Schuster, 1997.

Jankowski, Ben. "In Search of American Alt." *Zymurgy*, Winter 1994 (Vol. 17, No. 5).

Johnson, Sam. "An Easy-to-Build Mashing System for Precise Temperature Control." *Brewing Techniques*, July/August 1995 (Vol. 3, No. 4).

Kaiser, A. "Praktische Hinweise zur Erzeugung von Altbieren." *Brauwelt*, August 1978 (Vol. 18, No. 33).

Keay, Diane. "Brewing Water." *Zymurgy*, Winter 1986 (Vol. 9, No. 5).

Kieninger, H. "Altbiere." *Brauwelt*, May 1980 (Vol. 120, No. 22).

King, Frank. *Beer Has a History*. London: Hutchinson's Scientific and Technical Publications, 1947.

Kitsock, Greg. "Once upon a Vine." *Zymurgy*, Special 1997 (Vol. 20, No. 4).

Koehler, Wolfram. "Lager Beer: A Brief History." *Zymurgy*, Special 1993 (Vol. 16, No. 4).

Kruger, Lyn. "The Inhibitory Effects of CO_2 on Yeast Metabolism and Fermentation." *The New Brewer*, November–December 1996 (Vol. 13, No. 6).

LaBenz, Marty. "Reverse Osmosis Water Purifiers." *Zymurgy*, Summer 1989 (Vol. 12, No. 2).

Leistad, Rog. *Yeast Culturing for the Homebrewer*, Ann Arbor, Mich.: G. W. Kent, 1983.

Lewis, Gregory. "Kiss of Hops." *The New Brewer*, July–August 1994 (Vol. 11, No. 4).

Lewis, Michael. *Stout*. Classic Beer Style Series No. 10. Boulder, Colo.: Brewers Publications, 1995.

Lohberg, Rolf. *Das große Lexikon vom Bier*. Ostfildern, Germany: Scripta, no date.

Lowry, Scott. "Give Your Yeast a Good Home." *Brew Your Own*, October 1996 (Vol. 2, No. 10).

Lutzen, Karl F., and Mark Stevens. *Brew Ware*. Pownal, Vt.: Storey Communications, 1996.

Mallett, John. "Small Brewers and Malt." *The New Brewer*, March–April 1994 (Vol. 11, No. 2).

Maronde, Curt. *Rund um das Bier*. Stuttgart, Germany: Steingrüben, 1969.

Miller, David. *Continental Pilsener*. Classic Beer Style Series No. 2. Boulder, Colo.: Brewers Publications, 1989.

———. "Trends in Water Treatment." *Zymurgy*, Summer 1989 (Vol. 12, No. 2).

Miranda, Mary, Stephen Ask, Jean-Xavier Guinard, and Michael Lewis. "Analysis and Evaluation of Commercial Brewer's Yeast." *Zymurgy*, Special 1989 (Vol. 12, No. 4).

Monk, Paul. "Yeast Nutrients in Brewing." *Zymurgy*, Special 1989 (Vol. 12, No. 4).

Morris, Rodney. "Isolation and Culture of Yeast from Bottle-Conditioned Beers." *Zymurgy*, Special 1989 (Vol. 12, No. 4).

Mosher, Randy. *The Brewer's Companion*. Seattle: Alephenalia Publications, 1994.

Müller, Kristiane, ed. *Düsseldorf*. Hong Kong: APA Publications, 1991.

Narziß, Ludwig. *Abriß der Bierbrauerei*, 5th ed. Stuttgart, Germany: Enke, 1986.

————. *Die Technologie der Malzbereitung,* 6th ed. Stuttgart, Germany: Enke, 1976.

————. *Die Technologie der Würzebereitung,* 7th ed. Stuttgart, Germany: Enke, 1992.

Noonan, Gregory. *Brewing Lager Beer.* Boulder, Colo.: Brewers Publications, 1986.

————. *New Brewing Lager Beer.* Boulder, Colo.: Brewers Publications, 1996.

————. *Scotch Ale.* Classic Beer Style Series No. 8. Boulder, Colo.: Brewers Publications, 1994.

Noonan, Gregory, Mikel Redman, and Scott Russell. *Brewer's Handbook.* Ann Arbor, Mich.: G. W. Kent, 1996.

O'Neil, Carol. "Extract Magic: From Field to Kettle." *Zymurgy,* Winter 1994 (Vol. 17, No. 5).

O'Rourke, Timothy. "Making the Most of Your Hops." *The New Brewer,* July–August 1994 (Vol. 11, No. 4).

————. "Making the Most of Your Malt." *The New Brewer,* March–April 1994 (Vol. 11, No. 2).

————. "Making the Most of Your Water." *The New Brewer,* January–February 1994 (Vol. 11, No. 1).

————. "What Ever Happened to Maturation?" *The New Brewer,* March–April 1995 (Vol. 12, No. 2).

————. "Yeast: Nature's Little Beer Maker." *The New Brewer,* September–October 1994 (Vol. 11, No. 2).

Papazian, Charlie. *The New Complete Joy of Home Brewing.* New York: Avon Books, 1991.

————. "Yeast: The Sorcerer's Apprentice." *Zymurgy,* Special 1989 (Vol. 12, No. 4).

Pasteur, Louis. *Etudes sur la biére.* Paris: Gauthier-Villars, 1876.

Protz, Roger. *The Ultimate Encyclopedia of Beer.* New York: Smithmark Publishers, 1995.

Rajotte, Piérre. *Belgian Ale.* Classic Beer Style Series No. 6. Boulder, Colo.: Brewers Publications, 1992.

————. "Collecting and Reusing Live Brewer's Yeast." *Zymurgy*, Special 1989 (Vol. 12, No. 4).

————. "Collecting Yeast while Traveling." *Zymurgy*, Special 1989 (Vol. 12, No. 4).

Randel, H.W.G. "Altbier-Herstellung Heute." *Brauwelt*, August 1976 (Vol. 116, No. 33).

Reed, Gerald, and Tilak Nagodawthina. *Yeast Technology*. New York: Van Nostrand Reinhold, 1991.

Richman, Darryl. *Bock*. Classic Beer Style Series No. 9. Boulder, Colo.: Brewers Publications, 1994.

————. "Running a Yeast Test." *Zymurgy*, Special 1989 (Vol. 12, No. 4).

————. "Water Treatment: How to Calculate Salt Adjustment." *Zymurgy*, Winter 1989 (Vol. 12, No. 5).

Rodin, Jon, and Glenn Colon-Bonet. "Beer from Water." *Zymurgy*, Winter 1991 (Vol. 14, No. 5).

Rümmler, Else. *Zum Uerige: Past and Present*, 2nd ed. Düsseldorf, Germany: Josef und Christa Schnitzler, 1985.

Scheer, Fred. "The Danger of Using Two Different Yeast Cultures in Fermentation." *The New Brewer*, November–December 1996 (Vol. 13, No. 6).

Schloßbauverein Burg an der Wupper. *Adels Schloß und Ritter Burg*, 4th ed. Essen, Germany: Thales, 1995.

Schumann, Uwe-Jens. *Deutschland Deine Biere*. München, Germany: Zaber Sandmann, 1993.

Sillner, Leo. *Das Buch vom Bier*. München, Germany: Feder-Verlag, 1962.

Thomas, David, and Geoffrey Palmer. "Malt." *The New Brewer*, March–April 1994 (Vol. 11, No. 2).

Thomas, Virginia. "Barley Is the Heart of Beer." *The New Brewer*, March–April 1994 (Vol. 11, No. 2).

Tubs, Jerry. "Incorporating Activated Carbon Filtration in the Brew Process." *The New Brewer*, November–December 1996 (Vol. 13, No. 6).

Walz, Greg. "Boiling Methods and Techniques." *Zymurgy*, Winter 1987 (Vol. 10, No. 5).

Warner, Eric. "The Art and Science of Decoction Mashing." *Zymurgy*, Special 1993 (Vol. 16, No. 4).

―――. *German Wheat Beer*. Classic Beer Style Series No. 7. Boulder, Colo.: Brewers Publications, 1992.

―――. "Malting Techniques." *Zymurgy*, Special 1993 (Vol. 16, No. 4).

―――. "An Overview of the German Brewing History." *Zymurgy*, Special 1993 (Vol. 16, No. 4).

Woods, Melinda. "Yeast: Use It or Lose It." *The New Brewer*, September–October 1994 (Vol. 11, No. 2).

Index

American Society of Brewing
  Chemists, SRM and, 125
Aroma: flavor and, 43;
  strength of, 84
Aroma hops, 35, 45, 47, 98,
  99; adding, 44, 83-84
Aschaffenburg, alt from, 30
Astringents, 45
Autolysis, 88

Bacteria, 61, 62, 122
Barley, 36, 37
Bavaria, alts from, 42
Bavarian brewers, lagers and,
  11-12
Beta acids, 44
Beta-amylase, 1, 27, 28
Beta-glucan, 76
Bicarbonates, 41, 120; alka-
  linity and, 121
BierKeller malt, 34
Bittering hops, 43, 83; calcu-
  lating, 98-99, 130-37;
  low-alpha/high-alpha, 135;
  neutral, 45-46; North
  American, 46; trace ele-
  ments in, 137
Bitterness, 44, 134; up-front,

28; water hardness and, 137
Black malt, 68, 69
Blonde malt, 36
Body, 68
Boiling, 3, 53, 70, 79-82, 97;
  adding hops during, 43-44;
  time for, 80
Bottles, swing-top, wire-bale,
  91 (photo)
Bottom-fermented beers, 19
Brauerei Ferdinand Schu-
  macher, x, 19
Brewing, 6, 67-91; city/coun-
  try, 12-13; summer, 11
Brewing liquor, 42, 98
Brewpubs, altbier, 25-26
Brews, tribal, 6-8
Briess Malting Company, 34
Bronze Age, beermaking in, 6,
  9
Brunswick, alt from, 29
Burghers, ale making by, 13,
  14, 15

Calcium, 41; alkalinity and,
  121; mash pH and, 120
Calcium carbonate, 41, 42, 120
Calcium hydroxide, 41

Index

About the Author

Horst Dornbusch was born and raised in Düsseldorf, Germany, home of Germany's altbier. In 1969, he came to the United States on a Fulbright grant and earned a B.A. from Reed College in sociology and an M.A. from Brandeis University in politics.

Dornbusch liked life in the New World—except for the beers. Not surprisingly, he decided to become a homebrewer and make his own. With very little written material available in English at the time to guide him, he began studying the standard texts  of German master-brewer programs to learn how he could duplicate in his own kitchen the taste of real beer.

After a twenty-year career in broadcasting, editing, and publishing in the United States and Canada, Dornbusch enlisted as a volunteer weekend apprentice at the Ipswich Brewing Company in Massachusetts, where he learned to make beer on a commercial scale. In 1995, he started his own contract brewing company specializing in German-style beers. One of his company's flagship beers is—what else?—Dornbusch Alt, an authentic Düsseldorf-style brew.

In his spare time, Dornbusch combines his love of beer and words by lecturing and writing about brewing and the appreciation of beer. He is the author of *Prost!: The Story of German Beer* (Brewers Publications 1997), a humorous account of the history of German beer from its murky beginnings among the Germanic tribes of the Bronze Age to the sophisticated lagers and ales of the present day.